"*Multiplication Moves* provides a practical framework to help churches actively engage the process of starting new congregations, from motivation to implementation. God designed the church to grow and multiply. May the tribe of church-planting churches increase. Don't just read this book—do it!"

—Dr. Bob Logan, president of Logan Leadership

"Wow! I've known Ben Ingebretson to be a great thinker, leader, and writer—and in *Multiplication Moves* he's done it again. This is a persuasive, readable, and extremely practical guide for leaders who are open to seeing their church reproduce. Thanks, Ben, for helping us take the next step in expanding God's kingdom!"

—Dr. Tom Nebel, director of church planting, Converge Worldwide

"*Multiplication Moves* is a practical guide for teams who want to see the advance of the kingdom of God through church planting. Ben helpfully guides readers through the fine details of what it takes to plant a church. I pray that through this book, and others like it, God will stir the hearts of his people to see every tongue confess Jesus as Lord.

—Dr. Ed Stetzer, president of LifeWay Research

Foreword by Rich DeVos

Multiplication Moves

Ben Ingebretson

With Paul DeVries and Jim Poit

A Field Guide for Churches Parenting Churches

FAITH
ALIVE®
Christian Resources

Grand Rapids, Michigan

Library of Congress Cataloging-in-Publication Data

Ingebretson, Ben.
   Multiplication moves: a field guide for churches planting churches / Ben Ingebretson with Paul DeVries and Jim Poit; foreword by Rich DeVos.
       p. cm.
   ISBN 978-1-59255-726-4 (alk. paper)
   1. Church development, New. I. DeVries, Paul. II. Poit, Jim. III. Title.
   BV652.24.I54   2012
   254'.1—dc23

                                                                    2012002498

10 9 8 7 6 5 4 3 2 1

MIX
Paper from
responsible sources
FSC® C011935
FSC
www.fsc.org

Dedication

This book is dedicated to church multiplication teams at the local, regional, and national levels who seek to stir up a vision and practice of parenting churches—in particular, the Church Multiplication Initiative of the Christian Reformed Church and the Reformed Church in America. We are stronger together!

Contents

Foreword

I'm excited about the topic of this book: planting new churches. Starting any endeavor can be daunting, but I can point to a number of thriving, vibrant churches in my home community of Grand Rapids, Michigan, that were church plants just a few years ago. From my experience as a successful entrepreneur, I also have learned that the best approach to any new venture is to let your dreams overcome your doubts and just get going.

You might question my comparison of starting a church to starting a business, but there are many similarities. Both require sound fundamentals: a vision, a plan, leadership, a dedicated team, good workers, and a commitment to succeed. In fact, when I was starting out in business, I gave a motivational speech to my team called "White Heat." I told them that success in their businesses would require the same white heat passion demonstrated by the apostle Paul as he traveled around the Mediterranean to spread the gospel and start Christian churches.

I think this book will help inspire that same passion among those contemplating planting churches, help them overcome any doubts, and provide a clear roadmap.

Before you get into the book, let me share some thoughts on what you might want to watch for as you lead a congregation into a multiplication move. I call it "The Four Stages," and it's a dangerous cycle that any organization can fall into. When the church changes from an organization concerned with evangelism to one of "busy work," it is going through these four stages. They are the building stage, the managing stage, the defending stage, and the blaming stage.

Every church, including yours, started with the building stage: an exciting and challenging time of creating something from nothing, getting out and talking with people, encouraging them to be part of a new church community, and inspiring growth.

Next is the managing stage: after achieving some success, more energy is focused on internal matters like finances, budget, staffing, titles, offices, and musicians. Much more time is spent in the office with people coming to you to solve their problems—and, as a result, growth slows.

In the defending stage, the primary concern becomes justifying what already has been gained and staying busy with staffing, counseling, visiting the sick, and conducting funerals. The church spends more time "feeding the flock" and little time reaching new converts.

The blaming stage is when the energies of the group are turned inward, and defending the lack of growth becomes much more personal. It typically results in members bickering among themselves, blaming others for the church not growing, and forgetting what it's like to be out there creating and building from nothing.

Church planters can look forward to the excitement and rewards of creating, and their focus will naturally be on evangelism. I salute them for that. But I hope new and older congregations will recognize when the excitement of creation might start getting bogged down in organization or sidetracked by defending or division. If you start to sense the downward spiral of these other stages, you have a simple answer: go back to stage one. Refocus on your original purpose. Get out and start winning new people for Christ and start new churches!

I was thrilled when I was asked in 2009 to speak at a joint conference of Christian Reformed and Reformed Church pastors who were seeking a stronger, more unified witness to the gospel of Jesus Christ. I heartily applaud all efforts to multiply churches and reach more people with this Good News. We need to combine efforts to introduce more new believers and seekers, most of whom likely are not even aware of the history of denominational differences but are simply inspired to worship God together. Through established and new churches, we can engage our communities together and aspire to be a strong and unified Reformed voice that is relevant in today's culture.

If you picked up this book because you were serious about knowing the best practices of church planting, I thank you and I admire your mission and conviction. With this knowledge and God's help, you will have everything needed to get started. My experience and advice have always been that you can never wait until you have all the education, wisdom, and knowledge you think you need to get started. Sooner or later, you need the courage and conviction to just do it. And I know you can do it!

May God bless you and guide you as you embark on his purpose of spreading the Good News.

—Rich DeVos

Introduction

"Are you an accidental diminisher?" That question came to me in a book by Liz Wiseman titled *Multipliers: How the Best Leaders Make Everyone Smarter* (HarperCollins, 2010). I quickly browsed the contents and made my way to the back of the book, where I found a link to an online assessment of my "multiplication quotient." The self-assessment drew me in like a powerful magnet. In hindsight, I should have known I would be provoked by the question of whether I was an accidental diminisher. It pokes at something deep in the soul.

"Generativity" is a word developmental psychologists use to describe a phase of our human journey. Erik Erikson first used the term in the 1950s to describe a maturity level that comes when we are eager to see others thrive, not just ourselves. Erikson understood the human developmental process to be a series of conflicts. On our life journey we eventually come to the conflict of generativity versus stagnation, according to Erikson. Do we focus our energies and our accumulated wisdom on the next generation, or do we fiercely hold on to what we have?

Obviously, our best contributions are those of giving away our wisdom, handing off new opportunities, distributing precious resources, and releasing our energy to those better prepared to take a leap into the future. We may have climbed mountains and crossed divides, but one day it becomes clear to us that we might not take the next territory. Like Moses, we look over Jordan and see a great opportunity, recognizing that sending new leaders off to make the next advance is our best hope. Our new role is to launch them. That is generativity.

The alternate pathway Erikson labels as "stagnation." Like a pool of water with nothing new coming in or flowing out, we grow fetid, hoarding resources, clutching opportunity, keeping ourselves at center stage. In so doing we become diminishers of the next generation or the next visionary poised to stand on our shoulders and surge ahead.

From a developmental perspective, generativity is a natural and predictable life stage to enter and experience. I believe it is also a level of spiritual maturity that can develop without respect to our age. Tom De Vries, general secretary of the Reformed Church in America, pointed out that Jesus challenges us to ". . . go and bear fruit—fruit that will last" (John 15:16). These words must have sounded strange to the disciples, who knew that fruit has a short shelf life. After providing various reasons why fruit does not "last" (it gets eaten by ravenous teens or health-conscious adults or, if left alone, it eventually rots), Tom said that the only way fruit can last is through the seeds it produces. When we open our eyes, we see generativity all around us in God's design.

Generativity is not only a developmental task we are designed for; it is the example of Jesus, who wants to see lasting fruitfulness and who trained up his disciples and then released them, saying, "All authority in heaven and on earth has been given to me. Therefore go and make disciples of all nations, baptizing them in the name of the Father and of the Son and of the Holy Spirit" (Matt. 28:18, 19) and ". . . Whoever believes in me will do the works I have been doing, and they will do even greater things than these, because I am going to the Father" (John 14:12). Jesus showed us what generativity looks like!

Up Close and Personal

One of my greatest joys is working with pastors who challenge each other to walk boldly in the path of Jesus and move toward multiplication. Peter, for example, is a pastor of a declining urban congregation that has faced the fact that it will likely not survive. The neighborhood around the church is changing, and dramatic action is needed. Peter is a young leader who does not chronologically fit the "generativity" life stage described by Erik Erikson. Still, he has made it his passion to find a leader who does fit the changing milieu of the church neighborhood and set that person up for success in "nesting" a new congregation within the congregation's existing building. Peter is committed to making a multiplication move, knowing full well the new congregation will probably outshine the group he pastors. I marvel at his maturity.

Multipliers are unique leaders. Liz Wiseman analyzed the practices that distinguish 150 leaders and found a number of areas in which multipliers differ from diminishers. Her list of "The Five Disciplines of a Multiplier" can be summed up this way:

- ❯ Attract and optimize talent. The diminisher is an empire builder. The multiplier is a talent magnet.
- ❯ Create intensity that requires best thinking. The diminisher is a tyrant. The multiplier is a liberator.
- ❯ Extend challenges. The diminisher is a know-it-all. The multiplier is a challenger.
- ❯ Debate decisions. The diminisher is a decision maker. The multiplier is a debate maker.
- ❯ Instill ownership and accountability. The diminisher is a micromanager. The multiplier is an investor.

—from *Multipliers*, pp. 21-22

It isn't hard to see how these qualities relate to ministry leaders who are serious about being on mission with Jesus. Our Savior embodied many of the qualities identified by Wiseman's research.

This book is intended to motivate and empower leaders to multiply their congregations. No two situations are identical, so read it as a collection of best practices that your church will probably need to engage if you want to multiply churches. They're not meant to be a wooden sequence of exercises but a collection of suggestions based on a broad cross-section of multiplication experiences.

Ministry presents too many variables and surprises for us to "lock in" a one-size-fits-all multiplication process. Our hope is that you can use these chapters as tools for planning a multiplication project and as a guide for leading your congregation. This book can help you align your team, engage thinking, and lead your church into a multiplication experience. At a deeper level, however, this book is about living gratefully in God's grace and blessing, so that we open our hands and release our resources into the harvest God will gather unto himself.

I am grateful for the Church Multiplication Initiative of the Christian Reformed Church and Reformed Church in America, which has made this book possible. Special thanks go to Leonard Vander Zee and Sandy Swartzentruber for their care and skill in editing the text. I also am thankful for Jim Poit and Paul DeVries, who tested each of these chapters in our monthly church parenting webinar. You'll see notes from them throughout. Without their partnership, this book would not be possible.

—Ben Ingebretson

Chapter 1

Mapping Your Starting Point

"I do things I have never done before so that I might learn how to do them."
—Pablo Picasso

When my friend Dan gets a smile on his face he lights up the room, and on this occasion his smile was nearly blinding. Dan had felt a deep call to move his congregation toward planting another church but wondered how to share that call with the leadership team. One day he discovered a written history that revealed that the church had parented multiple congregations over the years. So birthing a new congregation was not alien to the church, as Dan had thought it was; that vital history was simply unknown to the current members. Dan had found his leverage point, and the smile on his face seemed to predict a favorable turn.

Many leadership teams considering a multiplication move through church planting are in settings where there is no collective memory of church planting. They ask, "We have never done this before—where would we begin?" Just as an athlete is able to move instinctively through muscle memory, it is possible for an organization to move with confidence using organizational memory. But, given time and leadership turnover, that memory often becomes dull or altogether lost. The thought of church planting seems risky. Parenting seems like a herculean effort rather than a reflex.

Whether or not church multiplication is part of the history of your congregation, it is certainly part of the DNA of the church of Jesus Christ. The book of Acts tells us that the first church of Antioch prayerfully deployed church planting missionaries to Cyprus (Acts 13). That was the beginning of a multiplication move that, within a few hundred years, resulted in Christianity saturating the Roman Empire. Churches planting churches was God's original pattern. It begins with one disciple making another disciple, as Paul coached Timothy: "The things you have heard me say in the presence of many witnesses entrust to reliable people who will also be qualified to teach others" (2 Tim. 2:2). The multiplication of believers leads to the multiplication of leaders, ministries, and congregations.

When this natural multiplication movement becomes the domain of denominations and agencies rather than the local church body, the local muscle memory is lost. Today there is a strong movement to return to the local congregation as the prime agency in church planting. We are getting back to multiplication!

Where do we start? On our knees? For sure. With a planter? In time. Reaching underserved people? Of course. Facing our "risk avoidance"? Yes. There are all kinds of strategies and no shortage of pitfalls; this is not a linear, assembly-line process. However, we have discovered through experience that certain tasks need to be accomplished in order to successfully birth a new congregation, and there is a common (though not rigid) sequence to those tasks.

As with any endeavor, the first step can be the toughest. What is *your* starting point? This question is one we can all wrestle with, though leaders, and particularly the lead pastor, must especially engage here. In this initial chapter we take a look at a few guiding questions to help you discover that starting point for your congregation. The answers you give will help you plot your present position and discern your next steps.

What Is Your Commitment Level?

In my conversations with leaders and congregational teams who are exploring parenting a new church, the question of commitment surfaces early. It comes down to this: how deeply are you devoted to the vision of a new church, and what are you willing to do to achieve that outcome? What are your deepest commitments in ministry? I first ask this question of the leadership, not the congregation.

Peter Senge captures this question in a powerful way when he says, "Ultimately, leaders intent on building shared visions must be willing to continually share their *personal visions*. They must be prepared to ask, 'Will you follow me?'" (*The Fifth Discipline*, Doubleday, 1990, p. 200). We are talking here about the "fire in your belly." This is where leadership begins. I have never seen successful church parenting apart from a lead pastor who is committed to it. Parenting is not, first of all, about a time frame to pull it off or a particular method to make it happen or the problems and attitudes we will face. The single most crucial factor for churches planting churches is a God-inspired vision that has a taproot into our soul and spirit.

What are your core commitments? This is a good question for the pastor, but it applies to anyone with leadership responsibilities. If you are fortunate to serve with others who share your desire to parent a new church, you will benefit from their developing support. If not, you will need to dig a deep well to feed your heart and mind as you wait on others to catch the vision. You will need to seek God's power through prayer. Books and colleagues can provoke you toward multiplication, but it takes time with God to sustain your vision and burn a contagious leadership commitment into your spirit. There is no other way to sift your core values and ignite your soul. Church planting is God's mission, and entering that mission means that we need to seek God's face. Prayer will not only be a screen that sifts your motives, values, and priorities; it will also be a place where God will meet you and speak to you from the heart of his mission.

Having this vision does not mean that you will have all the answers or see a clear path to follow. It does mean that you will have a picture of a preferred future to pursue with God's help. When a leader or leadership team is clear and united in commitment to the vision God has for them, a spark ignites into a flame. Neglecting to gain clarity about your values and the commitment level required for church planting can easily lead to failure down the road.

From Paul

My first pastoral experience in church planting was a failure. Although the leadership of our congregation agreed to be the calling church for the pastor of a new church plant, we never did anything to build or develop a system of values, a rationale, or a prayerful commitment for church planting. Even as I agreed to serve as a pastoral mentor for the planter, there was no clear vision and certainly no unified support. In short, we simply said "Yes" without ever mapping out the commitment level or developing the values necessary for such an endeavor to be blessed. Not surprisingly, the plant and the pastor both struggled. In hindsight, it is clear that our failure to be more proactive and patient in developing a shared commitment and energy for planting hindered the ministry from the start.

Developing clear-headed commitment to the vision by congregational leadership is step one. The next question relates to the kind of ministry environment that leaders and congregation share. Getting the answer right makes the difference between a faltering and a flowing parenting experience.

What Is Your Trust Quotient?

Parenting a new ministry stirs up plenty of anxiety in people. They will ask questions like these: Will people leave our church? Why we are doing this crazy thing? Where will the new ministry be located? How will we pay for it? and on and on. In order to embark on what seems like a risky venture, people need steady, trustworthy leaders and lead teams who are walking closely with God. Building trust is, therefore, part of the advance work leaders need to accomplish before they cast a vision or move out into action.

In his excellent book *The Speed of Trust* (Free Press, 2006, p. xxii), Stephen Covey outlines a series of trust-building moves that can have a profound impact on progress. They include these:

- talk straight
- demonstrate respect
- create transparency
- right wrongs
- show loyalty
- deliver results
- get better
- confront reality
- clarify expectations
- practice accountability
- listen first
- keep commitments
- extend trust.

This list makes it clear that building trust takes time. It also reveals the importance of a *mutual* trust between two parties—in this case between leaders and their congregations. Parenting church pastor Paul DeVries says that, in his experience, too many leaders lack trust in those they lead, even while asking the congregation to trust them. Likewise, leaders too often demand commitment to their vision, while failing to give the same commitment in return. Simply put, to get trust and commitment you have to give trust and commitment.

But what does that look like? This is where Covey's list comes in. As you read through the list, ask yourself whether it describes how leadership individuals and teams in your church relate to the congregation. If not, you now know where to start. None of us will be perfect in this, but we should be working on the process of trust development. Building trust is a foundation to leading a congregation through a high-impact multiplication move like parenting a new church. The level of trust is also an indicator of your starting point. This is a good place to turn off your clock and make trust a goal unto itself for a season. When you have confirmation that trust runs deep between your leadership and the congregation, you may be ready to take the next step.

Can You Focus on the Process?

There are usually two approaches to leadership that pulse just below the surface when congregations contemplate a multiplication move. In almost every board, council, or consistory room that I visit, these two perspectives compete for priority.

One perspective insists that before any action is taken every question be answered, every detail addressed, and every potential outcome anticipated. Until all the possibilities have been dealt with, there is no willingness to commit to the goal. The problem with this approach is that the number of variables involved in planting a church makes it impossible to move ahead at all.

The alternate approach involves working through the process one step at a time, moving ahead unless and until something happens that requires a stop. Some call this "building the bridge while we cross it." It is not an excuse for carelessness, but it does hold open some future decisions. For example, a congregation may proceed with a church planting project without knowing who the planter will be, because they are not yet ready to search and make a hire. A lot of important groundwork can and will take place before any church knows who its church planter will be or what shape the plant will take. Insisting on seeing every detail of the project from the beginning will douse many good sparks of the Spirit in church planting. Completing each step, one at a time, produces a forward momentum to the next step in the process. It's the difference between making a commitment to the whole project in one moment versus making a deliberate commitment to the process.

Being a parent church will probably stretch your faith like never before. For most, those earliest steps in the process seem most difficult. Like a rocket breaks the restraining force of gravity at liftoff, congregations can feel like they are moving at a snail's pace while expending great energy. One helpful reality is that, unlike biological birthing, the incubation time in church parenting can be slowed or accelerated based on how the process is going and on the church's overall readiness. Early steps in the process do not necessarily lock us in to exact timelines or outcomes. The option of a "pause" in the process almost always exists, up until the planter is hired and finite prelaunch funding sources begin to be used. That said, commitment to the process means moving ahead whenever possible.

Will You "Stick It Out"?

The next question applies especially to the senior pastor and is particularly critical in midsized or smaller congregations where there is solo pastoral leadership: is the pastor committed to staying with the parenting project until the church plant is launched?

Some time ago I was coaching a pastor who was seeking to lead the congregation toward parenting, but he was actively exploring another ministry call at the same time. Parenting a new church does not absolutely demand that the same pastor champion the cause from start to finish, but in most cases that is best. As mentioned previously, the process of parenting can be "paused" at several early junctures. For example, if a parent church experiences a pastoral transition during the year prior to hiring the planter and releasing the core group, pausing the process is probably wise.

The process of parenting, from the dream through to the release of a new church plant, is a two- to four-year experience for most first-time parenting congregations. A senior leader who commits to staying with the parenting congregation through the entire experience, particularly if it is their first planting experience, significantly increases the chances for a positive outcome.

Who Will Support the Parenting Vision?

A Native American proverb says, "If you seek to make a fast journey, travel alone. But if you seek to make a long journey, travel with others." Parenting a new church is, more often than not, a longer journey than expected. It takes longer to align leadership, longer to prepare the parenting congregation, longer to find the right planter, longer to arrive at a winning strategy, and longer to raise the needed funds than first expected. Given the likelihood of a long haul, it's crucial to build a good team to travel with along the way.

A few trusted core leaders may be united in this vision at the start, or you may be standing alone with the dream. Whatever the case, it is critical to recruit and develop others who will share the parenting church vision. For most it will begin in the circles of influence closest to the congregation's leadership, such as other formal leaders in the church. Then there are also the "informal" leaders, who carry considerable weight in many congregations. They may have held leadership roles in the past, or they may simply command the respect of their fellow congregation members. In one congregation I served we stood poised to parent a new ministry, but there was lots of hesitation in the congregation. Bob, an older former council leader, had had a positive experience many years back with church planting. When he spoke to support the vision, it carried a lot of weight! When Bob shared the transforming effect that church planting had made in his life, people sat up and listened.

From Paul

A friend once asked me, "Was the church plant your idea or Dirk's idea?" Dirk is our congregation's church planter. He had been serving with us as a staff person. He rose up from within our church with his planting dream and tipped the opinion scales toward parenting. I answered, "Well, I think it was God's idea and then my vision, but ultimately it was Dirk's presence within the congregation that made it all come together." In other words, sometimes a certain individual comes along at just the right time, with just the right gifts, and with a willing heart and spirit—and that individual will win the commitment of others. If God presents you with such a person, praise God and walk through the open door!

Another sphere of potential partners would be colleagues and ministry peers who have either parented in the past or are supportive of your vision. Fellow congregational leaders from diverse settings who pull for one another can bolster a sagging vision. For some leaders, a network of learning, support, and accountability is exactly what they need to keep pressing toward the multiplication vision. As a member of my network commented, "I want to do this, but I need the discipline of others to keep me focused."

The reality is that congregations naturally turn inward over time, which lessens the time and energy they spend on outward focus and action. A group of kindred spirits who spark each other's vision and hold each other accountable is often a crucial component in moving against the gravitational pull of congregational inwardness.

One smart strategy is to engage one or two "partner parent" congregations in your efforts, as those who could learn from your lead parenting role. They would be asked to consider a commitment of finances or people to help out. Triad parenting can be very effective when one takes the lead and others help where they can as "apprentice parents." The result is a stronger support for the new church and additional future parent churches.

Finally, consultants and denominational leaders can help keep the vision alive. Because they are aware of the pitfalls and mistakes of the parenting process, they can offer seasoned insights. They can help in gathering the resources necessary for the task—and this is no small matter. Today, more than ever, denominations are giving prime energy to church plant staffing and resourcing. Don't miss out on these experienced counselors!

With a network of supportive partners in place, you can plot more precisely your starting point in parenting. Ideally you have support in each sphere I have outlined: formal and informal leaders in your church, area pastors and leadership peers, denominational consultants and coaches. If not, you might need to widen your partnership circle. In the coming chapters you will gain some insights into how to do that. In the long run, that wider circle will help you go farther down the road to a successful parenting experience.

How Does the Parent Assess?

Assessment is a critical element in church planting, and is usually thought of in relation to the church planter: is he or she right for the job? The same question should be asked of the parent. Parenting a new church may be your deep desire, but there are factors that can give you an early indication as to whether doing so is wise or not.

The following indicators should give you pause as a potential parent:

- ❯ General poor congregational health. Parenting out of pain is rarely a good idea, as it is likely to cause large numbers of people to flee the parent church. Church splits are not God's design for kingdom advancement! Healthy congregations are united in the Great Commission and Great Commandment. They are multiplying believers, leaders, and ministries.

- ❯ Attendance decline. Parenting usually involves the home congregation sending off people (ideally 40 adults) to form a core group to launch the new church. Churches that have declining attendance are likely to be damaged by that loss of people. Starting a second, alternate-style service or nesting a new congregation within the walls of the parent may be better ways to respond to a declining congregation.

- ❯ Financial stress. Parenting usually involves providing funding help to the new church. Doing so can tax givers at the sending church beyond their capacity; the loss of offerings from those who leave to form the core group can also be a blow. While it is important for the parent church to help provide funding when needed (see Chapter 5), it is also important to not overextend the parent church financially.

The following indicators should give you a nudge forward to parent:

- ❯ Your ministry is seeing evidence of multiplication. New vision, new believers, new leaders, and new ministries are springing up. If your congregation is already holding multiple services, that demonstrates that sub-multiplication (disciples, leaders, ministries) is already taking place.

- ❯ Underleveraged resources are evident. "Asset mapping" is a great exercise to use to identify financial, facility, creative, and volunteer assets that could be used in a church plant. Perhaps you have leaders who are underchallenged. Ministry "bench strength" is a great thing until those who are on the bench begin to feel they never see the field!

- ❯ Multiplication values are evident in your congregation. When your existing values are congruent with the values that tend to identify a parenting church, you are likely to parent naturally with little impact on the health of your congregation. Those values are likely to motivate your leadership to align easily around a parenting methodology. Check out the Values Assessment scale in Appendix B, and see Chapter 4 where those values are identified.

Where Is God Moving?

Our greatest challenge is to find out where God is moving and get on board. This is especially true in the vision of parenting a new church. You and I can read the best demographic studies of our communities, interview the most successful church planters and multiplying leaders, read all the books, and attend conferences—and we *should* do all those things. But there is no substitute for quiet reflection and listening in prayer before the Lord.

There is a striking expression that echoes through the book of Acts: "It seemed good to us and to the Holy Spirit. . . ." Practicing collective spiritual discernment from the earliest stages should be the goal. When done humbly, spiritual discernment aligns leadership and bends personal agendas toward God's purposes.

Where is God moving in your community? To answer that question, do some spiritual mapping by asking these questions:

- Where do you see redemption, health, and wholeness?
- Where do you see brokenness, division, struggle, or godlessness?
- What is the pulse of other key spiritual leaders? Where are they seeing hope?
- Where is significant change taking place? What changes do you see in neighborhoods, businesses, entertainment, ethnicity, population, family structure? All are indicators of a community's spiritual geography.
- What is proving effective in other ministries in the community? Without being hostage to fashion, what can you humbly learn and accept as local ministry wisdom from other ministry leaders?

Discovering where God is at work in your community requires seeking out people who are not in your normal relational "bandwidth." Bill Easum describes how for several years he regularly visited a local pub so he could stay grounded with the people who were in his community and hear their questions and concerns. In so doing he was better able to see how the Spirit was working.

One of the most remarkable trends in North America is the dramatic infusion of ethnic groups from across the world, and the significant Christian presence they bring. Immigration is fueling a remarkable upsurge of vibrant ethnic evangelical church planting! One noted observer writes, "Contrary to popular opinion, the church is not dying in America; it is alive and well, but it is alive and well among the immigrant and ethnic minority communities and not among the majority white churches in the United States" (Soong-Chan Rah in *The Next Evangelicalism*, InterVarsity Press, 2009, p. 14). How might we participate in this? God is moving here, and wise congregations move according to what "seems good to us and the Holy Spirit." Can we partner with Christian immigrants to help plant new churches?

Spiritual mapping is also necessary within your congregation. Perhaps a season of listening will help you discern a new vision that God is growing. There may be an awareness in your church that members are "not getting any younger" and it is time to explore new ways to steward the resources of your ministry to match that new vision. While movements of God sometimes begin quietly behind the scenes, they can also be dramatic, ear splitting, turbulent, and even stormy (read Psalm 29). The history of the church includes many stories of how the Spirit shook things loose! Might this not happen in our day too? Whether it's in careful and measured steps or in dramatic moves, the question is always What is God doing here?

Sometimes we can discover where God is moving in the community by noticing who is *not* entering our church doors. Established congregations often underestimate how difficult it is for new folks to feel comfortable and welcome. The patterns, practices, and social groups of any existing congregation can be an insurmountable barrier for some—even when the church goes out of its way to be inviting and enfolding. Are there individuals and groups within your community that your congregation isn't reaching? Perhaps discerning God's movement and will means that your congregation needs a new ministry to reach those people. Or perhaps the best solution is to birth a new congregation with fresh focus to reach an underserved group.

It's all about prioritizing God's mission. It is not the pastor's mission, nor is it the mission of the council or the denomination. This is God's mission.

What does God desire for us at this moment? For the pastor, elders, and deacons this begins with discerning where God is moving within them. What is God pressing into their hearts? God calls us to love with all our heart, soul, mind, and strength. In a place of surrender and availability we can listen and perhaps hear a fresh word . . . a confirming word . . . a challenging word.

We don't have a choice as to where we start. We all start this journey in the same place: right where we are today. Recognizing your starting point can help you slow down and do the best foundational work, whether that includes deepening commitment, growing trust, expanding the sphere of support, or discerning God's movement. A healthy multiplication move grows up from cultivated soil. From here, with God's call and the Spirit's power, we can move forward!

Next Step Questions

1. What level of commitment do you have to being a multiplying leader? How have you engaged prayer to anchor this commitment in your heart and ministry?

2. What trust building needs to be done before you attempt to lead the congregation into a major multiplication move?

3. How committed are you and your team to working within the multiplication process?

4. Who are your immediate and potential partners in parenting? List them. Who might you add?

5. Where is God moving in your community and congregation? How might you discern that more deeply going forward?

Chapter 2

Making the Case to Parent

"If you wish to win a man over to your ideas, first make him your friend."
—Abraham Lincoln

My pastor friend Tim was "gung ho" for church planting when a growing midsized Midwestern congregation interviewed him for the lead pastor role. The church was poised to begin a new building project as its ministry continued to expand, but Tim challenged the congregation to look in another direction: parenting a new church. People politely listened and evidently overlooked some of their skepticism, and the church hired him.

After settling in and earning some credibility, Tim began to risk his "leadership chips" in conversation about parenting a new church. But a multiplication move made absolutely no sense to his leadership team. There were plenty of existing churches around, and they had heard a few horror stories of church plants that did not pan out. And, of course, the church was growing, as evidenced by its expanding campus.

Tim joined me and a handful of other pastors in my office one day to talk about church planting. As we talked, we knew that "making the case" would be a key tipping point for his church. After several months of our meetings he still did not see a way forward. But then the leaders of Tim's congregation made a remarkable 180-degree change in their attitude toward parenting as a result of a compelling set of facts, a gripping opportunity, and a credible appeal, as you'll see later on in this chapter.

Aristotle taught that persuasion requires three elements. The first is *logos*, or basic information. Depending on your audience, appealing to reason and commonly known information is critical in making the case to parent. Next, Aristotle commends to us *pathos*—an appeal to the heart that connects with our passions and convictions. Sometimes just one story about a person who came to Christ through a new church can be very persuasive for fence-sitters. Finally, Aristotle commends *ethos*. This is the credibility and trustworthiness that lie in the character of the communicator. *Ethos* is the moral weight we carry by virtue of what people think of our faith-based leadership. Together, *logos, pathos,* and *ethos* are powerful forces in persuasion. When these elements pervade the leadership team, they will help make a compelling case for church parenting in your congregation.

The emphasis of this chapter is on the *logos* aspect—making a rational case to parent—but your team should not neglect developing an appeal to the heart and establishing your credibility as leaders. Demographics and statistics, strategic planning and stewardship, biblical and pragmatic thinking all can come into play when laying out a reason for making a multiplication move. When *logos* is coupled with *pathos* (an appeal to the heart) and *ethos* (credible messengers) there is potential to help people take a step into alignment with God's mission of church multiplication.

Making a Biblical Case to Parent a New Church

For Christians, the vision for church planting begins with the Bible itself and the picture it gives us of the very nature of God. The triune God—Father, Son, and Holy Spirit—has called us to join in his mission, and that mission is the basis for church multiplication.

God the Father is a missionary God.

Beginning in Genesis 12 God is described as being on a mission to bless all the peoples of the earth. "The LORD had said to Abram, 'Go from your country, your people and your father's household to the land I will show you. I will make of you a great nation, and I will bless you; I will make your name great, and you will be a blessing. I will bless those who bless you, and whoever curses you I will curse; and all peoples on earth will be blessed through you'" (vv.1-3). The idea of "blessing" occurs five times in this text, and the unmistakable message is that God intends to bless the peoples of the earth through blessing Abram.

Moving to the New Testament, Peter picks up on the blessing of Abram, saying, "And you are heirs of the prophets and of the covenant God made with your fathers. He said to Abraham, 'Through your offspring all peoples on earth will be blessed.' When God raised up his servant, he sent him first to you to bless you by turning each of you from your wicked ways" (Acts 3:25-26). In this text we see that God remains on a mission to bless people through sending Jesus Christ and through calling out a people to be agents of his blessing.

With the choosing of Abram and Israel, the biblical doctrine of God's election brings into focus the missionary purpose of God and our relationship to it. Our election is for the purpose of God's mission. Jesus said to his disciples, "You did not choose me, but I chose you and appointed you so that you might go and bear fruit—fruit that will last."

The late Lesslie Newbigin, a theologian and missionary to India, gives us this insight into God's electing purpose:

> And we can also see that whenever the missionary character of the doctrine of election is forgotten; whenever it is forgotten that we are chosen in order to be sent; whenever the minds of believers are concerned more to probe backwards from their election into the reasons for it in the secret counsel of God than to press forward from their election to the purpose of it, which is that they should be Christ's ambassadors and witnesses to the ends of the earth; whenever men think that the purpose of election is their own salvation rather than the salvation of the world; then God's people have betrayed their trust (*Household of God: Lectures on the Nature of the Church*, SCM Press, 1953, p. 55).

God has chosen the church to send it into the world to bring blessing. This missionary purpose of God is at the core of church planting.

Jesus Christ sends us to plant his Word in the lives of people.

The New Testament gives us four "commissions" from the mouth of Jesus that tie us into the missionary work of God:

> "As the Father has sent me, I am sending you." (John 20:21)

> "Go and make disciples of all nations, baptizing them . . . " (Matt. 28:19)

> "Repentance for the forgiveness of sins will be preached . . . to all nations." (Luke 24:47, TNIV)

> "You will be my witnesses in Jerusalem, and in all Judea and Samaria, and to the ends of the earth." (Acts 1:8)

Each commission gives us a deeper understanding of the mission on which God sends us. It is worth noting that Tim Keller sees in the Great Commission (Matt. 28:19) an often-overlooked call by Jesus to plant new churches. Keller argues that baptism in Acts and elsewhere means the incorporation of an individual into a worshipping community with accountability and boundaries (see Acts 2:41-47). Jesus calls us to baptize, knowing that doing so requires the formation of communities. The only way to be truly sure you are increasing the number of Christians in a town is to increase the number of churches. Traditional evangelistic work may get "decisions for Christ," but only when people are enveloped into a believing community are they likely to persist in their faith. (Keller's compelling case to plant churches can be found online at tinyurl.com/RedeemerPlant.)

These commissions, taken together with the words of Jesus "I will build my church" (Matt. 16:18) locate the impetus for church planting with our Lord himself. The church is the only institution Jesus has promised to build. He does not construct this building with stones or steel; rather, he builds it through the people he transforms through encounters with the life-changing power of his Word. Jesus is the builder. This is not the only metaphor Jesus gives us, however.

In a parable that is repeated in each of the synoptic gospels (Matt. 13, Mark 4, and Luke 8), Jesus gives us another rich metaphor of the power of the Word to transform people; "Listen then to what the parable of the sower means: When anyone hears the message about the kingdom and does not understand it, the evil one comes and snatches away what was sown in their heart. . . . But the seed falling on good soil refers to someone who hears the word and understands it. This is the one who produces a crop, yielding a hundred, sixty, or thirty times what was sown" (Matt. 13:18, 23).

A key element of our work of blessing is to plant the seed of the Word of God in the lives of people such that it bears much fruit. This is the foundation of church planting. Paul picks up on this metaphor in 1 Corinthians 3:5-15, where he describes his work as a church planter. Writing about the multiple factors that went into the formation of the church at Corinth, he states, "I planted the seed" (v. 6).

Jesus' commissioning words, his promise to build the church, and his power to transform lives through the Word are key biblical reasons to plant new churches.

The Holy Spirit empowers us to start new churches.

Luke begins Acts by referring to his gospel as the things "that Jesus began to do and to teach" (Acts 1:1). In Acts we see what Jesus continues to do and to teach by the power of the Holy Spirit. As soon as the Spirit descends on the apostles, we see that what Jesus is about is building a church that will bring the blessing of the gospel to the ends of the earth. God has chosen and called the church to be the primary vehicle for that mission. Acts shows us the work of the Holy Spirit in a tremendous advance of this blessing through church planting.

The central figure of the whole book is the apostle Paul. Most of us think about Paul as a great theologian and preacher. We may also know of his missionary travels and leadership development of Timothy and others. We sometimes forget, though, that church planting was his passion and his life's work. Eckhard Schnabel writes, "Paul knows himself to be called by God to work as a pioneer missionary who 'plants' churches, who lays the foundation as an 'expert master builder,' that is, who establishes new communities of believers" (*Paul the Missionary*, InterVarsity Press, 2008, p. 152).

Paul gave priority in his life to this pioneer work, saying, "It has always been my ambition to preach the gospel where Christ was not known, so that I would not be building on someone else's foundation" (Rom. 15:20). Paul had an inclination to press outward, an urge that is still felt in the hearts of church planters today.

Before Paul, the planting of new churches to reach new people had already taken root. In Acts 11 and 13 we can read about the remarkable group of early believers who took the message of Jesus to the Greek-speaking people in a new place they had settled (11:19-20). That planting effort gave birth to a wonderfully diverse community in Antioch (13:1-2) that had a missionary spirit and a desire to multiply itself (13:3).

Paul saw himself as one of the apostles and was recognized as such by others. The word *apostle* means "one sent to bring a message," and it was also the word Jesus used after rising from the dead: "As the Father has sent me, I am sending you" (John 20:21). While the word *apostle* had the specific meaning of one who has seen the risen Lord, it was also used by Paul and others to refer to those who partnered with Paul in his apostolic ministry. Barnabas, Andronicus, Junia, and others were also referred to as apostles, and in Ephesians 4:11 Paul names the apostles as one of the gifts of the ascended Lord to his church, along with prophets, evangelists, pastors, and teachers.

In parenting and planting churches today we continue that apostolic ministry. When, like Paul, we urgently, prayerfully, and strategically embrace the call to join God's mission of bringing the blessing of the gospel to unreached cities and neighborhoods, tribes and peoples, we too may be counted as "outstanding among the apostles" (Rom. 16:7).

The story of the early church and of Paul's ministry offers a fascinating study in the dynamics, hard work, and priority of church planting. Reading through the book of Acts carefully and prayerfully may be exactly the place to start for your leadership team. The church moves out in ever-increasing effectiveness as it raises up new leaders and sends them out to plant new churches. Acts 19 pictures Paul lecturing daily in Ephesus, raising up disciples of Jesus who then fanned out throughout the province of Asia such that "all the Jews and Greeks . . . heard the word of the Lord" (vv. 9-10). It seems that Paul was training evangelists and church planters who could multiply his teaching and preaching ministry and thereby accelerate the gospel expansion. A remarkable multiplication move for sure! Planting churches was the Spirit's strategy to accomplish God's mission and still is.

Making a Sociological and Statistical Case to Parent a New Church

While we start with a biblical foundation for church multiplication, there are often discernable reasons why God works in the ways he does. Adding sociological data to the biblical call strengthens the case and helps open people's hearts and minds to parenting a new church.

My source for the following information is Dr. Dave Olson, the founder of The American Church Research Project (www.theamericanchurch.org) and the author of *The American Church in Crisis* (Zondervan, 2008). Olson's "Case for Church Planting" is an excellent free downloadable resource that offers a more detailed accounting of the discussion that follows. His data is based on a nationwide study of 305,000 churches, representing the great majority of Protestant, Catholic, and Orthodox Christians. Statistics on African American denominations and independent churches are more difficult to discern as they do not publish data, though the Glenmary study (www.glenmary.org) has sought to measure their presence also. Another very current study was completed by the Hartford Institute for Religious Research and can be found online at www.faithcommunitiestoday.org.

Here are six key factors that Dave Olson outlines:

1. The percentage of regular church attendance in North America is significantly overstated. Many people casually report church attendance of forty percent or higher in regions we think of as the "Bible Belt." Olson and others, however, say that a "halo effect" causes people to over-report behaviors that are considered desirable. (Ask a teenage boy how many times he has kissed a girl, and you will likely get the same phenomenon!) Olson cites studies that identify the "halo effect" on church attendance, saying,

> These studies indicate a rather large halo effect for self-reported church attendance. How much higher are the polls than the actual attendance count? The research of the American Church Research Project shows that 17.5 percent of the population attended an orthodox Christian church on any given weekend in 2005. (*The American Church in Crisis*, pp. 28-29)

Olson has graphed his findings as follows:

Percentage of the Population Attending Church on Any Given Weekend in 2005

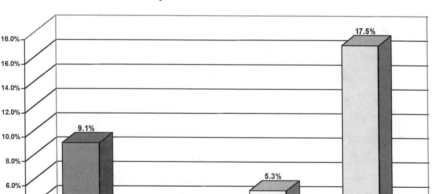

—from *The American Church in Crisis*, Zondervan, 2008, p. 29. Used by permission.

A study released in 2011 by the Hartford Institute for Religious Research confirms and extends this negative trend:

> More than 1 in 4 American congregations had fewer than 50 in worship in 2010, and just under half had fewer than 100. Overall, median weekend worship attendance of your typical congregation dropped from 130 to 108 during the decade according to the FACT surveys. While it is true that the number of mega-churches roughly

doubled during the decade, they still only constitute about a half of one percent of all congregations in the U.S. And while it appears to be true they are attracting an ever bigger slice of the religious attendee pie, it is a bigger slice of a shrinking pie. ("A Decade of Change in American Congregations 2000-2010," faithcommunitiestoday.org)

Of course, there are county by county exceptions to a region, so your particular location may differ somewhat. Suffice it to say that the picture that most of us have of 30 to 50 percent of Americans filling churches on Sundays is simply not true. Canadian churches are well aware that their attendance rates are lower still.

From Jim

Many well-intentioned church leaders oppose the planting of new churches because "there are already enough churches to reach our community." I once attended a funeral reception where I casually mentioned to a relative my interest in church planting. This relative informed me that her community didn't need more churches because everyone she knew attended church. She assured me that her community, which was located in the Midwestern Bible Belt, had been thoroughly saturated with churches that were, in her words, "already effectively ministering to the needs of the community." However, upon further research I discovered that only 36% of her community attended church. Perception is not always reality.

2. The number of Americans claiming no religious affiliation is growing. According to the American Religious Identification Survey, the number of people who say they have no affiliation doubled from 1990 to 2009, and the number of Americans who self-identify as Christians has declined from 86% to 76% since 1990. Not only are we attending worship less frequently, we are increasingly not identifying ourselves as Christian. North America has been rightfully identified as a mission field worthy of the best mission strategies and methods, and this study confirms that fact. Planting a new generation of churches led by a new generation of leaders provides the opportunity to reach people who are not being served by existing congregations.

3. Population increase is not being met with adequate numbers of new churches. Another way to represent the decline in religious affiliation is to look at population increase relative to church attendance. While church attendance in North America may grow from 50 to 60 million in the next 40 years, that will do little to keep pace with population increase, which is projected to grow from 300 million to 400-plus million people in the same time frame.

Sociological data tells us that nearly 90 million new people populated the United States between 1990 and 2006. Though there were 40 million deaths, that is still a net gain of about 50 million people. If we accept a sustainable ratio of one church for every 1,000 people (meaning each church would average 170 people with a 17 percent attendance ratio), that means that, theoretically, an additional 50,000 churches were needed during that period—or 3,125 new churches a year. But during those years North America saw fewer than 2,000 new churches planted per year.

This need is heightened when we consider that every year nearly 2,000 churches will close in North America. At the very least, existing churches need the help of newly planted congregations to address this staggering mission opportunity.

The following graph gives a picture of this need.

1990 - 2006 Population Growth by Births, Immigration and Death

THE AMERICAN CHURCH
RESEARCH PROJECT

©2008 BY DAVID T. OLSON
WWW.THEAMERICANCHURCH.ORG

—from *The American Church in Crisis,* Zondervan, 2008, p. 35. Used by permission.

4. New churches reach unchurched people at a far greater rate than existing churches. Taken as a group, churches that are fewer than 15 years old are significantly more effective in reaching new people and enfolding them than are older churches. This is not always easy for existing congregations to hear. Believing they can change, churches will work hard to keep their evangelistic edge and remain permeable to outsiders. There are certainly many wonderful exceptions to the rule, but it is hard to argue with the pattern. Ed Stetzer, citing the research of Bruce McNichol, notes, "Churches under three years of age win an average of ten people for Christ every year for every one hundred members. Churches three to fifteen years of age win an average of five people per year for every one hundred church members. Churches over fifteen years of age win an average of three people per year for every one hundred members" (*Planting New Churches in a Postmodern Age*, Broadman and Holman, 2003, p. 6). Stetzer goes on to quote the often-repeated wisdom of C. Peter Wagner: "The single most effective evangelistic methodology under heaven is planting new churches."

Dave Olson graphs the evangelistic impact of churches over time in the following profile (*The American Church in Crisis*, Dave Olson, Zondervan, 2008, p. 83).

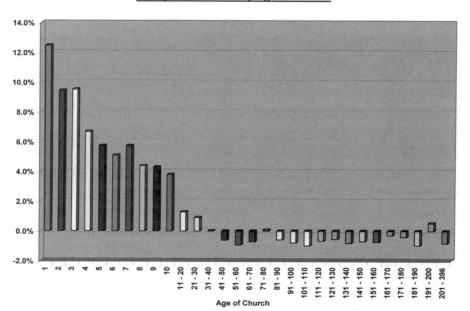

Yearly Growth Rate by Age of Church

—from *The American Church in Crisis*, Zondervan, 2008, p. 83. Used by permission.

Again, many well-meaning church leaders resist the idea of planting new churches within their communities because they would rather strengthen or revitalize existing churches so that they can be "retooled" for a new generation of believers. In his book *Forgotten Ways*, Allan Hirsch convincingly makes the case that the majority of churches, because of the way they conduct worship, the way they are organized, or what they espouse as their core values, have a "market appeal" for only 12 to 35 percent of the overall population. In other words, most evangelical churches today are competing for a very small slice of the population pie. They are unable to engage the wider community and intentionally draw the majority of its people into a deeper spiritual awareness of the presence of God. Hirsch writes:

> What is becoming increasingly clear is that if we are going to meaningfully reach this majority of people, we are not going to be able to do it by simply doing more of the same. And yet it seems that when faced with our problems of decline, we automatically reach for the latest church growth package to solve the problem— we seem to have nowhere else to go. But simply pumping up the programs, improving the music and audiovisual effects, or jiggering the ministry mix won't solve our missional crisis. Something far more fundamental is needed. (*Forgotten Ways*, Brazos Press, 2006, p. 37)

From Jim

New Hope Community Church is located in a large metropolitan area, and we consistently get visitors who have just moved into the area. Like most heavily populated areas, the community is transient. It seems that every week new visitors tell me how much they struggle to find a church.

One particular young woman explained that she was tired of visiting all the "vanilla churches" in town. I cautiously asked her what a "vanilla church" was. She explained that as a child she thought vanilla ice cream was too plain, especially because there were so many other exciting flavors to choose from. She said that the churches in our part of the city were all the same and they seemed unable or even unwilling to engage the culture around them in a meaningful way. They didn't seem interested in meeting her needs, let alone the needs of her unbelieving friends.

It will take a new church with a unique approach to reach people like this woman and her friends.

5. Increasing diversity is presenting a great opportunity to plant new churches. Ethnic change and immigration are bringing large numbers of new people to our communities and neighborhoods. These new people present a remarkable opportunity and need for church planting. For example, in North America the Hispanic community surged from 35 to 60 million people from 2000 to 2010. That remarkable growth alone should cause us to take a new look at our communities and their churches. Asian Americans and African Americans, along with countless other ethnic communities, are in need of a fresh wave of church plants.

My friend Jim and his wife, Martha, are a great example of a response to this change. Jim is Anglo and Martha is Hispanic. They shared a vision for their church to parent a new church along the lakeshore in West Michigan, where the number of Hispanic people is dramatically increasing and the community is underserved. With careful planning, a few years later they are celebrating not one but several new plants as the ministry to immigrants grows.

Another opportunity that indicates the need for planting new churches is generational change. Young adults are returning to live in urban centers, repopulate warehouse districts, and revive older neighborhoods. Mega-churches are giving way to smaller, sustainable churches where relationships are more personal. Meeting the needs of this rising generation and engaging its leaders can often best be accomplished by planting churches that meet their particular ways of being the church.

6. We are in an historic season of planting need. As we have seen, church planting is not a new idea. Church planting has been a primary means of growth from the beginning of Christian history. In the United States, the era of early Methodism and the eras following the Civil War and World War II were seasons of planting resurgence. Today we are witnessing a new season in which a number of factors converge, presenting new challenges and opportunities for evangelistic church planting. A sober recognition of the demographics and projections of church attendance in North America has mobilized many churches to see the need for planting new churches.

The church is finding its mission voice again as the wider culture drifts. Taken together, there is a sense that we are in a new updraft of spiritual hunger and church planting, such as has taken place in years past. At the same time, dozens of organizations, denominations, equipping agencies, and consulting and coaching services, as well as countless conferences, books, and tools have sprung up to aid and otherwise assist in accomplishing this calling in the coming years.

Again Dave Olson gives us a graph picture of the patterns of history and the season of need we are in:

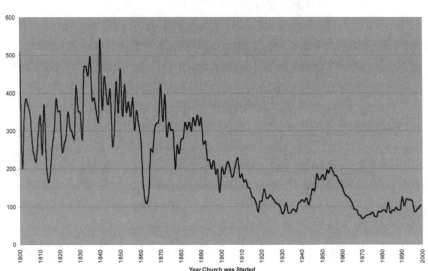

Churches Started per 1 Million Residents
Based on Start Dates of 92,677 Churches in the United States

—from *The American Church in Crisis,* Zondervan, 2008, p. 145. Used by permission.

The current need for new churches has been captured succinctly in the following church-to-population ratio declining sequence:

- ❯ In 1900, 27 churches existed for every 10,000 Americans.
- ❯ In 1950, 17 churches existed for every 10,000 Americans.
- ❯ In 1996, 11 churches existed for every 10,000 Americans.

—Tom Clegg and Tim Bird, *Lost in America: How You and Your Church Can Impact the World Next Door,* Group Publishers, 2001, p. 30.

The tools of sociology are useful in beginning to outline a case for church planting from the "outside in." Culture, history, demographics, and projections go a long way in catching our attention when considering a multiplication move.

My opening story about Pastor Tim and his Midwestern church is illustrative. Facing a lot of reluctance among his leadership council, Tim did some research and discovered both the need and an emerging opportunity to partner with a Hispanic church planter in his area. Armed with statistics about the number of underserved people in the church's community who did not speak English, the leadership caught the vision for a new mission opportunity that could only be met by planting a new church. After meeting the Hispanic planter who could be their partner, the leadership team and congregation are getting their feet wet in a multiplication move by supporting a Hispanic church plant.

It is the natural tendency of older churches to lose their mission fervor and begin to focus on their own internal needs. Congregations easily forget that they too were once church plants and that the first generation of believers upon which the existing ministry rests was, at one time, a "core group." Churches need to be reminded of their biblical heritage and their own history.

From Jim

A few years ago at Centerpoint Church in Kalamazoo, Michigan, the pastors felt God's call to begin planting a series of new congregations, but they knew that the church leaders would be hesitant. During one particular meeting the pastors had the leadership team reflect on the history of the church and write on individual sheets of paper all the significant events in the congregation's life. The pastors drew a timeline on the wall and had the elders and deacons tape their sheets of paper to the wall as they recalled each event.

When the exercise was finished everyone stood back with a sense of joy, seeing how the Spirit of God had led them over the years. They also noticed that at the beginning of their history, within a few short years of their own planting, God had used their church to plant other churches in their city. The church leadership discovered that church parenting had been part of their DNA from the very beginning. They realized that they stood in the tradition of the early church and of Paul's ministry. Needless to say, a new fervor for church planting arose in that room and the leadership prayed together, asking God how they could continue the tradition.

Making a Strategic Case to Parent a New Church

Tim Vink, the Reformed Church in America's coordinator for church multiplication, emphasizes the strategic importance of church planting. I have frequently heard him capture imaginations with an analogy drawn from the lives of senior adults he connects with. Multiplication makes the biggest impact in the third and fourth generations of a movement of new churches. This could take place inside of a decade as churches plant churches that plant churches (which seems to be Paul's vision in 2 Timothy 2:2).

Tim recently cited the story of a friend, Marv DeWitt, who had passed away in his ninety-second year with ninety-two descendants. His seven children had twenty-three grandchildren, who in turn had sixty-two great-grandchildren. Tim keenly observed that 85 (or 92 percent) of the children were part of the third and fourth generations! Multiplication is very powerful when compounded by time.

When new churches are planted with a vision to multiply themselves, there is the potential for a great gospel harvest in the future. What greater legacy could we leave than to bring into the harvest of history a reaping movement ordained by God to bring tens of thousands of people we will never meet into God's kingdom? When we think about using our time, talents, and treasure wisely, as good stewards who will one day give account, church planting seems to be a wise and strategic investment. Who knows—we may see that third or fourth generation in our lifetimes, adding joy to our journey and glory to God!

Making a Pragmatic Case to Parent a New Church

The best cases for church planting rest on a biblical foundation, sociological need, and strategic wisdom. But there are other reasons why planting should be seriously considered by every congregation:

1. Planting reactivates passive members. When your church moves into mission mode in planting a new church, people who have been sitting on the sidelines can "step up" in new ways. Countless churchgoers become conditioned to a passive mode because they simply feel that they are not needed. Musicians, teachers, accountants, and other willing hearts often disengage when they feel they aren't needed. Planting can change that quickly.

2. Planting brings to the surface new ministry methods for congregations that have stagnated. Because church plants have to reach new people with an old message, they are forced to think creatively about communication and effectiveness. They cannot just do what they have always done and expect a different outcome. In their active pursuit of relevant ministry to the community around them, they become a research and development laboratory for ministry change.

Parent churches are often revitalized through the energy and insights that surround church planting. Again and again I have seen churches that plant new congregations begin to see their own ministries sharpened. I have seen parenting churches reevaluate the effectiveness of their ministries to children and youth, and I have seen pastors reevaluate their preaching and the style of their worship. In this case Proverbs 27:17 rings true: "As iron sharpens iron, so one person sharpens another."

3. Planting a new church helps deploy maturing staff members. All too often, the natural upward maturity and growing capability of an existing youth pastor, associate pastor, or other staff member requires that they leave the ministry and find a new environment where their gifts are appreciated. Parenting a new church gives opportunity for staff to grow and take on new responsibilities that may fit their gifts and skill sets. At New Hope Community Church, our youth director has been attracting and mentoring several new young couples in our congregation, and he has many creative ideas for a new worship service that could reach this unreached demographic of our community. None of the parents want our youth director to leave, but if we don't challenge him and help him reach his potential, he *will* eventually look for other opportunities. The church leadership, therefore, wisely began to invest in him as a church planter. Of course, using staff members to plant churches calls for great care, as planter selection cannot be led by fondness for a staff member alone, but staff can be an excellent source for new leadership.

4. Planting is the most effective way for your congregation to do evangelism. The graph on page 36 from the American Church Research Project makes it clear that churches under ten years of age, taken as a group, are the most effective at evangelism. Planting a new church is an excellent way to get the biggest impact for the energy and resources invested. Another study completed by a large denomination confirmed the impact of church plants, finding that

❷ churches under three years of age averaged ten conversions per hundred members per year,

❷ churches three to fifteen years of age averaged five conversions per hundred members per year, and

❷ churches over fifteen years of age averaged under two conversions per hundred people per year.

—Craig Ott and Gene Wilson, *Global Church Planting*, Baker Books, 2011, p. 29.

5. Planting restores a healthy dimension to your congregation's lifecycle. In nature, most healthy organisms reproduce at some point. Churches that never birth a new church are prone to becoming unhealthy. They lose touch with a vital reason for their existence: to be a living expression of the kingdom of the God who desires to reach all people. Parenting a new church restores a sense of congregational health and vitality.

One pastor in central Iowa recalled how his congregation struggled to reach people who lived north of the freeway that divided their city. Even though the congregation was located just a few miles south of the freeway, it was difficult to get people from the north side to join them; there seemed to be some kind of psychological barrier. After much prayer, the church leadership decided to plant a new congregation on the north side of the freeway.

The pastor said that the hardest experience in all his years of ministry was trying to get the congregation that was south of the freeway to contribute (over and above their regular giving) to the northern site—a campus at which they would never worship. However, as the southern congregation caught the vision, they experienced a spiritual revival, and members became more and more active in the life of the church.

As churches plant other churches, members from the mother church become mature followers of Christ and begin to use their gifts for the greater kingdom.

Making the Case in the Hearts of People

Leaders often discover that "the issue was not really the issue." Sound familiar? It would be a big mistake to assume that simply confronting the issue of demographics is all that's needed to persuade churches to parent. Again, Aristotle reminds us that *logos* (basic facts) is not the only leverage point in making a case for parenting. *Pathos,* an appeal to the heart, is sometimes every bit as powerful and compelling as the facts. When the facts hit home, people pay attention.

There is probably no greater source of contagious passion for church planting than when young people hear a call to do a new thing for God. When this happens, it disarms most of us and speaks directly to our hearts. We all long to see our children following Christ, and that desire can be a real tipping point for parenting a new church. Young adults today, like those in generations before them who had significant struggles, are tired of business as usual. They want to be, in the words of Alex and Brett Harris, challenged to "do hard things" (*Do Hard Things: A Teenage Rebellion Against Low Expectations,* Multnomah, 2008). My own children yearn to see their local church not only saving souls but addressing people's needs. They want to see their local church responding to social ills, including environmental degradation, social injustice and inequity, racism, corporatization, cultural homogenization, and the job rat race.

Several years ago my sister attended a large church in Houston that was raising money for a new bell tower. The congregation was also trying to raise money for the youth group to go on a mission trip to a very poor country. The senior pastor stood in the pulpit one Sunday morning and encouraged the congregation to stop giving to the youth mission trip and to redirect their stewardship to the new bell tower, because the bell tower added to the beautification of their campus. My sister looked at her husband after hearing the pastor's words and said, "Next week we will be finding a new church."

There is a movement among young adults today to plant a whole new generation of churches whose focus is not on building more and bigger buildings but on the impact or difference that the local church is making in the lives of the people who live in its neighborhood. I recently heard a story of a church that was very active in the community through a variety of service projects. The pastor felt God's call to leave that church in order to serve another church someplace else. On the pastor's last Sunday, the mayor of the town showed up and asked to speak. The mayor turned to the pastor and said, "You can leave. You have our blessing." And then she turned to the congregation and said, "But *you* can't leave; we need you in this community." This kind of local impact brings a whole new air of credibility to a new generation of emerging leaders.

Finally, encouraging new believers to tell their stories is an excellent way to appeal to the hearts of people in your congregation. A man named John shared his story with me one day as I was visiting his planting pastor. He had recently been divorced and felt a deep spiritual hunger, as well as a debilitating shame. He could not bear to walk into an established church because he felt he was not good enough for that crowd. The new church start, however, was relatively humble; it met in a local daycare building. So John gave it a try. He met Jesus there, and his life was changed! If John could share his story at your church, I think people would consider church planting like never before.

Next Step Questions

1. How will your leadership make the case for church planting to other leaders, and then to the wider congregation?

2. Using Aristotle's persuasion formula, which element *(logos, pathos, ethos)* do you need to develop more deeply in making the case with your people?

3. What communication process and strategy would help your listeners be more open to the compelling case for church planting?

Chapter 3

Building a Lead Team and Engaging the Congregation

"I not only use all the brains I have, but all I can borrow." —*Woodrow Wilson*

I have a pastor friend who works way too hard. Don't get me wrong—I'm not minimizing his stellar work ethic. He thrives in ministry and is effective in many ways, but sometimes he takes on too much. A while back he was approached by a member of his congregation who, after having watched the church successfully parent, announced that if the church planted another church effectively he would likely make a significant gift toward future church plants. The financial offer had plenty of zeros, and so my pastor friend jumped into action; within a year he was leading the charge for another plant. Not much gets past this friend of mine, and I am grateful for his energy for church planting. Still, successful church planting requires a team effort.

Today, people in business and industry recognize the wisdom of having teams tackle large leadership challenges. Jon Katzenbach defines a team as "a small number of people with complementary skills who have a common purpose, a common set of specific performance goals, and a commonly agreed upon working approach for which they hold themselves mutually accountable" (*The Wisdom of Teams*, Harper Collins, 1993, pp. xix, xx)

A congregation with a fresh vision to parent can be tempted to think that all it needs is one or two experts, along with the staff, in order to lead the church into a multiplication move. But most of the recent research and actual experience demonstrate that a team effort is a huge factor in making a successful multiplication move. When we build ministry structures that support our ministry values, we raise the likelihood of long-term success. A lead team can do a great deal to uphold the value of planting amid all the other concerns of congregational life.

From Paul

At Brookside Christian Reformed Church in Grand Rapids, Michigan, we were blessed with a church planter and a supportive denomination and classis. We could have just sat back and watched the gifted church planter, along with a denominational consultant, do their thing. Wisely, however, we realized the need for a collaborative team to work with our planter in the development of the project. Drawing on the wisdom and experience of many leaders in the church community, we quickly developed a lead team. This team enabled our congregation to "own" the project in a much fuller and broader way than we could have if it were just the planter's baby.

Duties of a Lead Team

The lead team is a group that works together within the parenting church to move toward a church plant. Perhaps a better term might be "guiding coalition." This team is not the same as the core launch group that moves with the planter into the weekly planting work. It's a coalition of influential people who have the vision and the passion for church multiplication. They inspire and guide the parenting side of the planting project. They keep the energy and direction of the planting project alive and continue to work toward the goals long after the initial spark and enthusiasm have faded a bit.

In the Reformed tradition, the church council or consistory exercises primary leadership in the congregation. However, since the officers of the church focus on overall leadership, it is usually necessary for them to call and commission a smaller team specifically focused on the church planting effort. This team should probably include some of the elected leaders, and certainly the pastor(s), but also other members who are gifted and passionate about the church planting vision.

So what does the lead team do? Following are some specific duties:

- **Understand the overall scope and sequence of parenting.** While no two parenting experiences are identical, it is important that the lead team has a grasp of the best practices of parenting and an appreciation of the tasks associated with each phase so they can calibrate time, energy, and expectations. A helpful section called

"Action Steps for a Parenting Church" can be found in Appendix A of this book.

- **Work with the council/consistory/staff to shape the vision for being a parenting church.** The team may take the church's initial vision to a deeper and more developed level based on new leadership commitments or changing circumstances.

- **Cast a clear and compelling vision for a new church with the congregation.** This is likely to complement a vision already articulated by the lead pastor. The team serves as an ally to the pastor and the elected leadership, communicating the direction and deepening the congregation's vision.

- **Identify the target area, ethnic group, or micro-culture to be the proposed focus for the plant.** This will likely be done in collaboration with pastoral leadership. Any direction the team decides on should be held lightly, as the selection of the planter could change the focus.

- **Determine the best planting model from a range of options, including nesting, multisite, hiving off, or other.** Again, this will likely be done in conjunction with the pastoral staff and elders.

- **Develop a preliminary profile for the lead planter.** This profile may also change over time and with new information.

- **Provide leadership in assessing planter candidates.** Working with outside, objective assessors who will discern basic planting aptitude, the lead team is key to discerning the "fit" of a planter prospect relative to the context and culture you are targeting.

- **Develop a business plan and adequate funding for the plant by cultivating multiple sources, including denominational and individual sources.** The planter often has the responsibility of raising a certain amount of the funding needed to complete the resource package. The lead team can be a vital partner to the planter in helping him or her make contacts with potential givers.

- **Maintain communication with the council/consistory and the congregation for prayer, consultation, and updates.** It is essential that a strong and broad network of prayer partners support all elements and stages of the parenting project. The lead team takes a key role in this, particularly before planter selection.

- ❯ **Assist the planter in the formation of a core group for the new church start.** This can involve recruiting core group members and/or helping to screen potential members.
- ❯ **Monitor, support, advocate, problem solve, cheerlead, and empower whenever necessary.** Lead team members are the dedicated eyes and ears who carry the hopes and dreams and the thoughts and prayers of the new plant project until it is released from the parent.
- ❯ **Anchor the movement in prayer.** Encourage prayer at every stage. Insist that the first and last work of the team be prayer. This cannot be overstated. Lead team members are more than just "doers." They are those who wait on God for wisdom, direction, and blessing.

Clearly, the parenting lead team plays a significant leadership role. It is important, therefore, that they have the full support of the pastor and elected leaders, and that the wider congregation knows about their work and supports them in prayer. There is no better way to begin than with a public commissioning in a worship service.

Forming a Lead Team

Recently I was invited to coach a pastor who was contemplating a multiplication move. The church was about eight years old and already holding two services, with more than 500 attendees. They were multiplying in every way, and it was exciting to see them blossom with vision and energy. As we sat together for our first coaching session, I listened as the pastor told me of the original vision to multiply their church plant and how the time had come to announce their "pregnancy" to parent again. Because they were such a new church themselves, no one needed to be persuaded by a compelling case for church planting—they were ready to go!

As we talked about next steps, my friend concluded that what he needed to do was develop a lead team. He decided to begin the process by asking his elders to pray about this critical step, thereby building their readiness to trust and receive the leadership of the soon-to-form lead team. We recognized together that elders have many concerns on their plates, and that if the new initiative to parent were to receive the support it needed the elders had to feel that they were part of the team's formation. I feel sure that when my friend Jon sees a lead team in place for the new venture, it will be a strong and effective team that works closely with the elders of the church as a multiplication force.

Selecting the team is a significant step. In most cases a team of four to eight individuals will be able to do the work needed to move the project forward. The team should include people who are highly committed to the vision and values of your ministry as a potential parenting congregation. The team might also include one or more individuals who are not members of your church. After all, if you want to reach people whom you are not already impacting, their representation on the team may provide valuable insight and perspective. I am aware of one church that recently took this step. As an Anglo congregation, they sought to nest an African American congregation in their facility as a response to the changing makeup of their community. So they recruited an African American pastor from another congregation to join their lead team. They needed insight from a different perspective and were blessed by the insights the African American pastor brought to them.

The following are some core qualities that should mark at least some of the members of your team. Lead team members might include

- ❯ people who are respected by others in the congregation and beyond.
- ❯ people with recognized leadership gifts.
- ❯ those with administrative gifts and ability to follow up on tasks.
- ❯ people with financial expertise and ability to help develop donors.
- ❯ those with a passion for the target demographic the new church is seeking to reach.
- ❯ experienced denominational personnel or other consultants.
- ❯ people of diverse gender, ethnicity, and age.
- ❯ people who are gifted in communications and media.
- ❯ those who have a heartfelt desire to follow the leading of the Holy Spirit through prayer.

Since a multiplication move usually involves months or even years of patient work, lead team members must be able to make a long-term commitment to the process of parenting. In addition to a commitment of time, the team must be committed to submitting to Scripture and to the work of the Holy Spirit in, through, and around them. Lead teams usually report that while their work often comes in spurts, they average one to four hours a week either in meetings or in task work.

What is the best way to recruit such a team? Engaging the insights and affirmation of the elected leaders is an important step. In a few cases your church planter may already be on board (as in when the planter comes from within the congregation) and will play an integral role in recruiting the lead team. Time in prayer and reflection will likely bring names to mind.

From Paul

At Brookside Christian Reformed Church, the church planter was given permission to recruit the lead team from the "pond" of existing leaders. While it's common for various ministries within a congregation to jealously guard their volunteers and frown upon others who recruit them "away," we found the opposite happening. The senior pastor "talked up" the church plant from the pulpit, encouraging active and gifted members to get involved. At the same time, the planter himself cultivated relationships within the congregation, discerned gifts, and asked for commitments from those interested in serving during the initial planning stages. The result was the development of a pre-launch team that was extensively involved from the outset.

Developing Team Trust

Perhaps the most critical quality of a lead team is trust. A lead team will need to navigate challenging issues, including planter selection, funding, and core team development. Without deep mutual trust they are likely to shortcut a good decision-making process based on a need for premature peace and harmony.

Strong trust is the foundation of the passionate debate and disagreement (within the team meetings!) that lead to the very best decisions. Your lead team should know how to "storm, norm, and form" together in ways that are not fracturing but bonding. Patrick Lencioni's book *The Five Dysfunctions of a Team* (Jossey-Bass, 2002) gives solid insights into the need for trust in a team and how to facilitate it.

Developing trust takes some initial time and effort. Rather than getting right down to business, take a meeting or two to get to know one another, and learn each other's stories. Taking that time at the beginning enables each member to know the deep currents that are pulsing through the hearts of other members. Ask simple questions to be answered by each member, such as

- ❯ What were your growing up years or your early formative experiences in the church like?
- ❯ What things about the world or our community touch your heart most deeply, and why?
- ❯ What led you to serve on this team? What would a "win" look like for you?
- ❯ How can we pray for you in your work or family life?

Teams Take You Higher

In ten years of working with regional and local church multiplication teams, I have been impressed by how they take ministry to higher levels than it would reach under a lone ranger. One exemplary team is chaired by Jeff, a leader who wonderfully brings out the best in the other members. Jeff does not need to be the one with the best idea, which is one of the reasons people love his leadership. He shares the floor and asks questions rather than making pronouncements. Jeff keeps the doors open to new team members and maintains the team meetings through the times of great progress and the times of little advance. The result is a steady and strong stream of new church starts. When you identify your team leader, look for a person with the qualities of my friend Jeff.

The time and effort it takes to select and support a solid multiplication lead team always pays huge dividends in the end, when solid strategies, congregational support, and the energy to see the project through yield a thriving mission plant.

Engaging the Congregation

The purpose of a Lead Team is to lead the congregation into the exciting and fulfilling journey of parenting a church. Right from the start, therefore, a lead team must engage the interest, understanding, and excitement of the whole congregation in a multiplication move. Unless multiplication has always been a part of a congregation's DNA, "springing" the idea on a congregation after months of planning and preparation will likely backfire.

Also, in most congregations there are polity issues or bylaws that stipulate that certain kinds of decisions be placed before the congregation for at least an advisory vote. In most cases, a decision to parent a new congregation requires a vote, if for no other reason than for budgetary implications. In addition, and perhaps most important, the prayer support of the entire congregation is critical. Prayer moves the ministry forward as the Holy Spirit inspires a greater vision. Therefore, engaging the entire congregation in the discussion at the earliest stages will greatly enhance the movement.

In chapter 2 we laid a foundation for building a solid case for church parenting, including biblical, demographic, strategic, and pragmatic aspects. The following section will help you communicate the vision to the wider body, using the questions that will be uppermost in their minds. It is important to note that this congregational conversation is likely to take place over an extended period of time as you move from the general idea of church planting to the specifics of being a parenting church.

Question: Why is planting a new church necessary in our community?

Presenting the great need to plant new churches does not necessarily mean that your church should parent, and so it can be a less threatening way to begin the conversation. But sharing the general need for church planting is a good way to introduce the "what" before you suggest the "who." Using national and local statistics, along with stories of those impacted by a new church, is a great way to present the need. You may also want to introduce some of your thoughts about underserved people in the community, as will be discussed in chapter 6. This public move naturally leads to prayer for God to guide your congregation as you consider the community's needs.

Question: What is the unique opportunity before us to plant a church through parenting?

This question requires that you help the congregation see some new situations in your community to which church planting is a timely answer. The presence of a new, emerging leader with planting gifts and calling; a new financial resource; or a demographic change in the community are all examples of unique opportunities. This public communication positions your church to consider its response to the new opportunities.

Question: What is the plan or timeline for planting this new church?

At a later point in the process, after strategic issues have been discussed and significant resources identified, a leadership team may begin to share a tentative plan with the congregation. Be careful not to set out precise launch dates and events until you have had time to study and design the pre-launch phase. Public communication here would involve a call for prayer relative to resources, planter selection, and eventual core group/volunteer development.

Question: What will a plant cost us in time, talent, and treasure?

The cost of such a venture will be a key concern for a congregation. Sharing at least a tentative budget and a plan for raising the necessary resources begins to move the vision to reality. Informing the congregation how it will be included in the formal decision-making process will also alleviate some concerns. Of course, money always follows vision, and vision provokes generosity.

Question: Who will lead the plant, and what are his or her qualifications?

At some point you will be seeking and choosing a church planter. Presumably the congregation will also be involved in this process, especially in those churches where a congregational vote is necessary for issuing a call. Sharing the particular gifts of the planter, and inviting him or her to share the vision with the congregation, will spark further prayer and enthusiastic support.

Making a compelling case includes taking people through a line of reasoning that helps them embrace the sound and reasonable nature of the effort, as well as the calling of God. The ways the congregation is engaged should speak to the head with statistics and credible testimony, as well as to the heart with passion and commitment. When a "case for support" appeals mostly to the head or mostly to the heart, it tends to be less effective. Capture both and you will see the greatest results in terms of people responding.

Next Step Questions

1. Who might you want to begin to cultivate as possible lead team members?

2. If you already have a lead team in place, are any important qualities missing? Which? Who might you recruit to join the team and fill in those gaps?

3. How clear are you and the team on the purpose, authority, and duties
    of the lead team? How can you help them accomplish their varied tasks
    effectively?

4. How can you facilitate trust among your lead team members?

5. What process will you need to follow to effectively engage the support of
    the congregation?

Chapter 4

Navigating Hidden Forces

"A hidden connection is stronger than an obvious one." —Heraclitus

Over the years some remarkable resources and leaders have emerged to fuel the planting of new churches in North America. Some of these leaders are giants in terms of experience and wisdom. Their work has filled bookstore shelves, commanded conference platforms, and appeared online. Many pastors and leaders have received their seasoned input, redirected their own values, taken the challenge, and moved out with vigor to plant new churches. But many other pastors and leaders have not. In the past I have been mystified by this response gap, but I have come to understand the deep, unseen currents and forces that inhibit a multiplication move in a local church.

A pastor friend once invited me to spend time with his church's leadership team as they considered parenting a new church. I met with the team for an hour, was thanked politely, and went on my way. The next day I called the pastor, only to discover that after I left the meeting all the big questions came out . . . in the parking lot! Over the following months I spent several evenings with that leadership team. They would inch forward to the edge of their greatest fears and anxieties about birthing something new and then pull back. As a mid-urban congregation in a changing neighborhood with declining attendance, their anxiety centered on the question of whether they would survive a parenting move. "What will happen to *us*?" was a question that rang in their hearts and minds. I am happy to report that today they are on their way to joyfully nesting a new church in their building. But that did not happen easily. They had to face many unseen forces before any real progress could take place.

Hidden Fears

When I consult with congregational leadership groups considering a church plant, I'm sometimes unnerved by their quiet demeanor. They stare at me, at the carpet, or out a window. I have learned that, when faced with a new challenge or opportunity, it takes time for some people to discern exactly what it is that they are feeling, and that at first they may be just trying to take in the novelty of a new idea. But the more they listen and reflect, the more they begin to feel excitement or fear. Sometimes they feel the ground is shifting under their feet and they are losing control. A significant change is being considered, and they begin to glimpse how it will impact them. They may not label what they are feeling as "fear," but that's often what it is.

When talking about parenting a new church, as with any change, there is a list of common fears the congregation needs to face. As a leader it is critical that you begin to identify those fears within yourself and within the people you seek to lead. Anxiety may be reasonable or unreasonable, but it is definitely real! The first step forward is to acknowledge those feelings and put them "on the table" where you can look at them objectively. It is not uncommon for most of us to need some help from a friend or trusted coach in facing our fears. Finding a place of honesty and transparency is a critical first step. From there we can work toward finding the calm center God has for us as we seek to walk in his will.

While these fears can be expressed in various ways, some are common to congregations that are making their first multiplication move. The following is a list of these common fears and some helpful responses.

Fear #1: Our congregation will lose valuable leaders and friends to the new plant.

It is true that new opportunities for ministry can change a congregation's normal social patterns. If a church has tended to define itself as "one big happy family in the same room at 10 a.m. on Sunday," they will likely feel threatened by a biblical call to God's mission that upsets the patterns they are used to.

Jim Poit tells this story about the fear of loss:

Recently a young woman in my congregation approached me to voice her concern about our new church planting endeavor. She valued the mature discipling she was receiving and was concerned that all our church's key leaders would go to the new church plant. I gently reminded her of why the church exists, and I challenged her to work through her fears in the light of God's mission. The young woman began to pray about the new church plant, and the Spirit led her to be part of the core team for the new church plant. The new relationships that she is now developing in the community as the new church plant develops are remarkable.

As I watched this young woman's spiritual journey, I have come to recognize that loss is a powerful emotion and experience. Paying attention to that experience without denying it is important. However, if I had not challenged her and others in my congregation to value the kingdom and make it the top priority, the church would become stagnant and begin to spiral into decline.

Fear #2: Our congregation will be less significant or relevant compared to the new plant.

Some people in your congregation will be drawn to the new church because they feel it is a better "fit" for them. After all, there can be four or five different generations in one congregation at one time. As a parent, part of me really wants my kids to engage in the natural pattern of going out on their own. Another part of me resists that release. Your congregation may have many of the same feelings as you experience the growing pains of multiple generations under one roof. You may be challenged to release a core group to plant a new church. As a result of that release, the parenting congregation will likely come to rethink its own ministry methods and approach, based on the effectiveness of the new plant. Planting is, as mentioned earlier, a kind of "research and development" arm of the church. New plants must attract new people, who will be forced to rethink everything in light of that mission, and their experimentation can benefit the parent church.

We need many different styles of churches to appeal to people's vast array of ages and preferences. No church can be all things to all people. Your church can, however, be just as relevant and significant as the one you parent.

Fear #3: The new plant will fail or otherwise be a negative experience.

It is true that most plants do not grow to become large, sprawling ministries. A key national-average study reports, "At the one-year mark, average attendance of a new church is forty-one people. At the two-year mark, it is fifty-six. At the three-year mark, it's seventy-three. At the four year mark, it's eighty-four" (Ed Stetzer, *Viral Churches.* Jossey-Bass, 2010, p. 101).

Some plants struggle along, people become discouraged, and the plant ultimately doesn't make it. That can be a really disappointing experience. However, the church planting movement has matured in wisdom from years of experience. By leveraging that wisdom, parenting churches can remarkably improve their odds of success. With better church planter assessment, qualified coaching, and careful risk assessment, the success rate can reach 80 percent (see *Parent Church Landmines* by Ben Ingebretson and Tom Nebel, Church Smart, 2009, pp. 51ff).

One church I know of had a negative experience but used it as a learning occasion. They parented another church soon after the failed plant so that they could remember the mistakes they'd made and avoid making them again. The result was a positive and fruitful new church reaching new people. Today that parent congregation is poised to parent again, having learned from a failure and celebrated a success.

Fear #4: The cost of birthing a new congregation will cripple us financially.

It is true that parenting has a price tag, and often it isn't cheap. Most new church starts that will employ a full-time planter require more than $100,000 in outside funding. It may help to bear in mind that while you should have this money committed before you move forward, it will be disbursed over two to four years, so you need not have it all "in hand" to move ahead.

It is also important to note that there are a variety of funding partners who are likely to consider joining your efforts, including some "aunt and uncle" churches that want to help out, individual donors who are personally committed to the planter, and denominational sources.

Finally, don't underestimate the desire of your own people to "step up" to this opportunity. Most churches receive 3 to 4 percent of the giving potential of their people. As in a capital campaign, in which a congregation can be predicted to raise more than two times its annual budget, people may consider special offerings for this effort.

From Jim

At New Hope Community Church we find ourselves surrounded by "snowbirds"—retirees who come to Arizona in the winter months to escape the cold. As we began two church plants this year, our winter residents partnered with us and contributed a substantial amount of funding toward these new missions.

God has remarkable ways of providing resources through potential and unseen channels. Consider the many biblical examples of how God provided for the material needs of the kingdom, often from places unexpected and unforeseen. The story of the church throughout history displays how God will provide for those who earnestly seek to be partners in accomplishing his mission.

Fear #5: Inexperienced or unqualified people will be thrust into positions of responsibility too soon.

It is true that church planting will call for people to step up into new positions with responsibilities that will stretch them. New people will be needed to greet, keep the books, play instruments, prepare communion, share late evening leadership meetings, lead Bible studies, and staff the nursery.

Your ministry will enter a phase of accelerated leadership development at some stage, as open positions need to be filled. For some congregations this is an opportunity to develop a ministry leadership mentoring program in which each leader identifies and cultivates a person to be his or her eventual replacement. "I do, you watch," then "We do together," then "You do, I watch," and finally, "You do solo" is a simple formula that, when combined with coaching, can develop experienced and qualified leaders.

Of course, biblical qualifications are always a bottom line for elders and deacons. A new plant may need to borrow from your inactive leadership pool for a season. In time the Holy Spirit and the Word will raise up new spiritual leaders for the new church.

Parenting is an opportunity to create a "culture of multiplication" in your congregation. Don't just talk about multiplying *churches*; talk about multiplying *leadership* on every level, from church school teachers to sound technicians. One pastor recently told me that his church tells people who want to lead that they cannot leave a ministry until they have trained two or three other people to do the ministry just as well as or better than they have.

Fear #6: The planting effort represents a rejection or repudiation of the values and philosophy of our congregation.

Church planting results from a recognition that the parent church is inadequate, in and of itself, to reach all the unchurched people in the community. For years the church where I worshipped and served was a mega-church with a vast array of programs. Everything seemed big. Today, largely due to the preferences of my adolescent children, we worship at a small church in an urban context. I have come to appreciate firsthand the generational preferences and personalities that contribute to the rich variety of churches in North America today.

A new church need not be about rejection of the parent church. It should be about a new gospel witness in a new wineskin for a new generation, opportunity, or need. When my kids move out and away, I don't see that as a repudiation or rejection of my values. It's an authentic and developmentally appropriate attempt to anchor the values of family and faith in a new context and in a new way that is theirs. As they love to tell me, "It's all good, Dad!"

In this listing of common fears perhaps you can identify some of your own concerns. When entering this new venture it's important to acknowledge that fears are real. Facing that truth is part of facing the fear. Honestly engaging and responding to fear, while holding up the biblical call to "fear not," is very much a part of making a multiplication move.

Hidden Values

The book of Acts helps us identify the next hidden force to navigate: hidden values. Two churches—the one in Jerusalem and the one in Antioch—epitomize divergent value systems. The Jerusalem church values the Jewish culture and traditions, which are mediated through its centralized leadership. The Hebrew language and the covenant signs of circumcision and ceremonial laws create an air of privilege given to God's covenant people (Acts 2 and 15). The Antioch church focuses on the new mission to the Gentiles. It values diversity, indigenous Greek language and culture, and a dynamic development of leadership (Acts 11 and 13). These two churches remind us that organizational cultures in churches can differ widely and that strong values and priorities lie beneath the external forms that surround our ministries.

From many years of observation, Bob Logan and Steve Ogne have identified seven particular values that predict and undergird a multiplication move:

- ❂ **Compassion for the unchurched.** Caring enough about lost people that significant amounts of time and energy are invested to reach them.
- ❂ **Culturally relevant style.** A style of ministry that attracts and connects with seekers and addresses their needs.
- ❂ **Great Commission orientation.** Seeing ministry in terms of people needing to be reached, not in terms of financial or other limitations.
- ❂ **Development and release of leaders.** Actively giving away the best leaders to start new churches.
- ❂ **Confidence in God's ability.** Making bold plans, believing that where God leads, God will provide.
- ❂ **Kingdom perspective.** Encouraging new churches to start close to home, while seeking a worldwide harvest.
- ❂ **Generosity.** Freely releasing people and finances to start new churches.

(adapted from *Churches Planting Churches*, Church Smart, 1995, pp. 3-5)

From Jim

At Centerpoint Church in Kalamazoo, Michigan, we created a culture that encouraged us to consistently pray for unchurched people in our neighborhood. For example, we once used sticky notes to place the first names of unbelieving friends on the walls of our sanctuary. We also began lighting a candle during the worship service whenever a person gave his or her life to Christ, and we celebrated that decision by encouraging that person to offer a testimony during the worship service.

When we decided to participate in the "40 Days of Purpose" program, our coordinator challenged us to do something that would force us to truly have faith. We decided to order twice as many *40 Days of Purpose* books as our congregation would need, so we could give away books to all the new people God brought into the church for this program. Because of

God's faithfulness we saw many lives transformed and we gave away all the books.

In both these cases our efforts began to form and "reform" our values. The bottom line is that we always need to be cultivating the multiplication values in our churches if they are to be healthy, reproducing congregations.

How can you create a "values culture" that helps a multiplication movement grow in your church?

Every congregation has certain values that rise to the surface, as evidenced by their actual practice. Actions speak louder than words! Discerning the dominant values in your congregation can be done through informal interviewing or in a systematic manner (see the "Values Assessment Tool" in Appendix B). Realigning the values of your congregation around those that have been identified here can take place through preaching and teaching and through action steps and ministries that reinforce parenting values. Every time you make one of the seven multiplication values real in your congregation through some concrete action, you move closer to a kind of "tipping point" where birthing a new congregation seems natural and appropriate because it's in keeping with your values. Being a parenting church is not dependent upon perfect multiplication values, but having evidence of those values most certainly does help!

Hidden Resistance

I once saw a cartoon that pictured a person dozing off in church, along with others who were barely hanging in there. The caption underneath the picture simply read, "Bored Again Christians." I thought it a fitting reminder of what church can become when there is no compelling mission that moves us forward!

Actually, the church does not *have* a mission; it *is* a mission agency sent by our missionary God. So it can seem strange to us when a church digs in its heels to resist a multiplication move without apparent good reason. Perhaps the underlying motive is either hidden fear or hidden corrupt values. Or perhaps it is simply a desire to perpetuate the status quo.

Conventional wisdom says that while 25 percent of people may quickly adopt a new vision and 50 percent remain uncommitted until they are persuaded, the final 25 percent are likely to be persistently resistant. These folks will resist as a matter of principle, regardless of the strength of the proposal or process. Sometimes I hear leaders espouse a "100 percent" vote expectation before they move ahead in mission. In my experience that's often a big mistake, given the predictable likelihood of resistant voices. However, it is possible to move a large portion of the people in the middle 50 percent in the direction of a multiplication move if we pay attention to good process.

In his book *Leading Change* (Harvard Business School Press, 1996, p. 21), John Kotter sets out a good format for leading change in a resistant or change-averse culture. The eight-step model he advocates (with our added applications) is as follows:

1. Establish a sense of urgency. In chapter 2 we provided help for making the case for the importance of parenting. Other situations in your context that could help you make the case include changes in your community, a rising average age in the congregation, or emerging leadership with planting gifts.

2. Create a guiding coalition. We walked through the formation of a lead team as a guiding coalition in chapter 3. Change-resistant congregations are more likely to accept the persuasion of a diverse representative group than that of an individual or even a church staff.

3. Develop a vision and strategy. When the vision and strategy come from the guiding coalition and represent a wider base, you will advance your case significantly with resisters. The strategy, when sound and reasonably informed by wise council, will help answer questions from those who expect good planning.

4. Communicate the change vision. We looked at this closely in chapter 3, where we discussed engaging the congregation with your vision. Successful communication of your vision requires a good plan to include people in many environments where the vision can be heard and understood. Creativity in this area can be a big help.

5. Empower broad-based action. Moving ahead when the waters are not calm requires that your staff and key leaders are aligned and equipped to do their part. When staff and key leaders are not empowered and committed, the whole movement can be sabotaged by what the military calls "friendly fire."

6. Generate short-term wins. Consider a second service as a small step before a full-scale plant, or consider parenting partnerships before making a solo parenting move. There are many ways to achieve short-term wins before a major success. Another option is to take any of the multiplication values identified earlier in this chapter and give them a concrete expression in a new way, thereby taking a small step forward.

7. Consolidate gains and advance change. When you are able to add up several small steps—e.g., new believers, new leaders, new ministries, second services, new capabilities in your staff, new resources, new successes in outreach ministries—the winds of a change in the culture of your ministry will be evident.

8. Anchor new approaches in the culture. Becoming a multiplying congregation will seep deeply into your culture and become normative when you tell the multiplication stories and celebrate multiplication activity. Working to see that every staff and volunteer person sees the multiplication potential and pathway in their ministry area will also go a long way toward anchoring this way of being.

Multiplication moves are rarely simple or easy. In most cases they upset a remarkably balanced set of forces—some helping and some hindering—that have held the church together for years. That "force field" traps the congregation in a position that is very difficult to change when moving into new territory. Imagine an intricate mobile suspended from the ceiling of your sanctuary. Floating in perfect balance are staff energies, financial resources, volunteer talents and time, mental models of "church," youthful energy for change, wise counsel for security, programming expectations, and on the list goes. All of these factors in tandem represent a degree of "push and pull" that together maintains the delicate balance of values and activities that make up a ministry.

To dramatically change one of those factors or introduce a significant additional element tends to bring imbalance, and the result can be very unsettling. This is the hidden side of a multiplication move that will likely become visible as you move forward. Taking the needed time, and working through a careful and transparent process, will help you navigate these hidden forces with a positive outcome.

Hidden Power

All this talk about process may make it seem as though a multiplication movement can be accomplished within a corporate-like framework. We cannot overstate the fact that undergirding prayer is critical to a successful parenting experience. A Spirit-driven, gospel-focused multiplication movement will seek God's direction, yield to God's timing, ask God for the right planter, intercede for the unchurched, and constantly implore heaven for wisdom.

Church planting is spiritual warfare. It is a direct assault on the forces of our enemy. When we set out to reach new people with the truth of the risen Christ, we can expect temptations and setbacks. The book of Acts is full of this cycle of advance, retreat, and advance again. In prayer we stay connected to the Lord of the church and remain in the power of his resurrection. Following are some suggestions for prayer in the process of parenting a new church:

- Take "prayer walks" around the neighborhood in which you sense a call to plant.
- Create prayer cards for people to post on a fridge or mirror to encourage daily prayer.
- Pray in your worship services for the planter search.
- Through prayer, consecrate those who will be in the lead team or core group.
- Send prayer updates and progress reports by email for wide distribution.
- Develop a prayer team for daily and weekly intercession for the planter and the unchurched.
- Pray for discernment of hindering fears, healthy spiritual hearts, and healthy parenting values within the congregation.
- Through prayer, seek wisdom in discerning the best planting method.
- Pray for insight into cross-cultural issues and for new leaders to join the work.
- Pray for honesty and accuracy in discerning and selecting the planter and core group.

- ❷ Pray for relevant community ministries to open doors and hearts to the new ministry.
- ❷ Pray for new stewards and generous givers to support the ministry.

We hope this list will trigger your own ideas to stimulate prayer activity. There are many other ways to incorporate prayer into the process. One church planting team developed a prayer network through a recurring email communication (or listserv) that people began to forward to others. As the momentum grew, a sense of God's power and strength and wisdom coming to rest on the planting effort grew with it. As an unexpected blessing, people began to discover the church plant project, and some felt a call to join the effort and be part of the launch. This all confirms the old saying "Prayer changes things, and the first thing it changes is me." This hidden power is evident in many areas of ministry, and church planting is no exception!

Force Field Analysis

A popular adage says, "Your organization is precisely calibrated to give you exactly what you are getting." Those words have been quoted by a host of people, perhaps because they are so terribly convicting! Sometimes it is helpful to give your leaders an appreciation of the forces that try to hold your ministry in one place.

The field of social science has given us a tool to understand the current position of an organization relative to its goals. "Force field analysis" maps out the opposing forces that keep us locked into our current position. Those forces are balanced between "driving" or "helping" forces that propel us forward and "restraining" or "hindering" forces that hold us back. A helpful exercise in breaking loose is to look at the chart on page 69 and try to identify the driving and restraining forces in your parenting efforts.

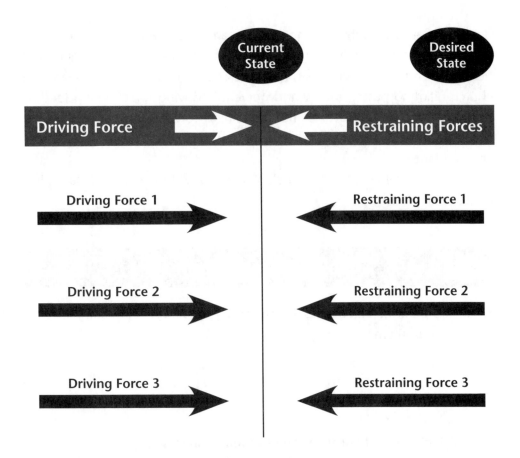

What driving and restraining forces are at work in your congregation? Driving forces might include congregational trust, clear vision, leaders committed to the vision, community need, resources, spiritual readiness, passion for the unchurched, availability of a planter, and more. On the restraining side you can identify fears, failures, resistance to change, lack of trust, distractions, absence of passion for the unchurched, no perceived need, and more. The effect of the exercise will be to give clarity on which factors need your attention. If the balance tips toward the driving forces, it is more likely your congregation will take a significant step toward a parenting move.

The "tipping point" for one church came when the pastor shared his vision with denominational partners. Upon hearing that the initial startup cost was a major restraining factor in enabling the church to move forward with the plant, both the denominational partners committed some of their funds toward the church planter's salary. With this assurance in hand, the pastor was able to go back to his congregation and significantly reduce one of the "restraining factors" that was holding the church back from the desired state of church planting. At the same time, a current member of the congregation was just graduating from seminary with the gifts and heart of a church planter. When he expressed his eagerness to serve as the church planting pastor, a new and powerful "driving force" was added to the equation. The removal of the restraining force, accompanied by the addition of the driving force, dramatically tipped the scales in favor of the church plant.

The "force field analysis" can help you at many steps along the parenting path. Use it often!

Next Step Questions

1. Which of the identified fears do you see in your setting? How can you begin to address them?

2. Which of the multiplication values is your church strongest in, and which ones do you need to grow in? How might you work with your staff or with others to "step up" action in those growth areas?

3. What level of resistance do you sense in your congregation? How might you measure that, and what action steps do you need to take to lead change?

4. What prayer strategies do you need to develop next?

5. How does the "force field analysis" help you map your way forward?

Chapter 5

Developing a Sustainable Funding Plan

"You can't always get what you want . . . you get what you need." —Mick Jagger

I recently looked at an online calculator that helps young couples project the costs of raising a child. The site asked for data on what part of the country the couple lives in, whether they have other children, and whether they plan to send their children to college. Taken together with other data, the calculator projected that it would cost nearly $150,000 to raise a child to age 18, with an additional $75,000 to put that child through college. I did this exercise at age 53, and my kids are all over the age of 18. I wonder what kind of family planning my wife and I would have done if I had consulted this website before our children were born!

Put bluntly, if people decided whether to have children based on a simple cost analysis, most would not. They just cost too much! Likewise, if churches only look at the financial cost of church planting, not many churches will be planted. But all parents, both of children and of church plants, will quickly testify that the natural benefits, joys, and blessings of having children are priceless. The benefits far outweigh the cost. Nonetheless, most young couples give thought to their ability to support a growing family before they create one.

When it comes to funding, many of us promote the "mammalian" philosophy of parenting new churches, as opposed to the "reptilian" form. This is the difference between significant or minimal parental support. Reptiles bear large broods of young with little regard for how many of those offspring live or die. Leatherback sea turtles, for instance, lay 100 to 150 eggs a season. Only a tiny percentage of those eggs survive seagull raids, predator fish, and a dozen other perils. The turtles simply lay their eggs in the sand, cover them up, and swim away. Mammals, however, bear fewer young at a time and usually go to great lengths to ensure their survival.

The very notion of being a "parent congregation" assumes some degree of care and support of the new plant to nurture it toward long-term survival. A significant part of that nurture is funding. In this chapter we look at the issue of funding from a variety of perspectives, with a goal of long-term sustainability.

What to Fund?

The process of putting a cost figure on a new church plant has changed a great deal over the years, as agencies and parent churches have refined an answer to the question "What should we fund?"

There was a time when local or regional denominational agencies would buy land that they would donate to a new church when it came of age. Business leaders and church leaders would evaluate community growth in a certain area and buy property when it was more affordable in anticipation of a future church plant. Later it became common for parent congregations to build a fund to help finance a worship center for a new church start. Sometimes that money was matched by denominations and others, leaving the new congregation with an affordable mortgage.

Those are interesting and, of course, helpful approaches, but they don't happen much anymore. The sheer number of churches that need to be planted in North America has created a new starting point in the discussion. Considering the cost of land and buildings, there would be very few starts per year if every start was given land and a building. We would definitely be taking a "mammalian" approach to church planting, and the number of plants would be miniscule. Today the focus is on planting a larger number of churches, which drastically changes the funding equation.

Most would agree that the single most critical funding recipient is the church planter. The right planter will, over time, reach people who bring their own financial resources to the mission for the purchase of land and buildings, as well as expanded programming and staffing. Part of the role of the planter is to develop new disciples who will become passionate supporters of the church—an activity that makes possible the planting of hundreds of new churches across North America. Funding the planter and some essential "startup" needs is the most strategic use of precious funding dollars.

This does not mean that providing support for buildings and property is poor parenting. When a new start is supporting its pastor and ministries but struggling to take the next step in acquiring property, it may be a great blessing to have outside support. Perhaps the congregation is mostly made up of people with modest incomes. While it is critical for the congregation to deeply "own" the decision to acquire property, there are ways to help with matching funds or interest-free loans. Help can be particularly beneficial if it does not interfere with the commitment by new church attendees to "step up" to the financial needs of the ministry. Capital campaigns are important seasons when the commitment level rises and ministry becomes laser-focused on growth. These are good qualities, for sure!

How Much to Fund?

Because no two church plants are alike, it is impossible to impose a precise funding plan on every plant. The staffing expectations, cost of living, experience and needs of the planter, the difficulty of the mission, and the presence of non-cash gifts are all variables that can significantly adjust the overall cost of the plant. Some plants are predetermined to be low-budget. Multisite and house church plants are far less expensive, in most cases, than classic congregating plants that employ a full-time pastor. There are, however, some key principles that can help you discern the degree of external funding needed in a new start. The following principles will help you determine the amount of outside support for the parent to plan on.

1. Agree on a balanced funding horizon.

The new church plant needs to be able to stand on its own two feet within a few years of its launch. External support has to be calculated to achieve this ultimate goal. Too much external funding, and the congregation will not develop the "muscle" of generosity and the discipleship of stewardship. The result is years of unhealthy economic dependency. Too little outside support, and the planter will be unable to focus on making new disciples and building a core of committed givers.

A good starting point in balanced funding is to limit outside funding to not less than two years or more than four years. Stephen Gray's research points out that

> in the second and fifth years, when financial support ended for church plants, significant differences were discovered. When a church plant's finances were cut off at the end of their second year of existence, there were 23.4 percent more fast-growing church plants than struggling ones. When a church plant's finances stopped at

the end of the fifth year of existence, there were 25.5 percent more struggling churches than growing.

—*Planting Fast-growing Churches*, Church Smart, 2007, p. 66.

External funding needs to be enough to get a church plant past the tough first two years but not into a fifth year, when economic dependency begins to set in. Plant funding is a delicate balance between too little and too much. Funding is like fertilizer—too much burns the harvest, while too little starves it.

The lesson here is that a long "funding runway" may give you a modest church plant, but probably not a strong one. Shorter runways tend to weed out weak plants, making it possible to give greater attention to the healthy, vibrant plants. It's important to come to agreement early about the funding runway you choose, so that it's clear from the start to both planter and parent.

2. Build a preliminary budget.

What will be the major overhead expenses that the new church will need to carry during the launch phase and the sustaining phase? Salaries for the pastor and key staff, advertising, worship space, and outreach programming are some major costs. Regarding staffing, in most cases the first staff addition will be a part-time worship leader and office help. Other significant "one-time" expenses can include media equipment, nursery items, tables and chairs, musical instruments, staging equipment, signage, and storage or a trailer. This is an area where the plant model you choose (see chapter 7) may significantly impact your costs. If your planter is bi-vocational and the model is one that uses donated space, your costs will likely be much less. It is important to remember, however, that bi-vocational pastors tend to plant churches that are smaller than those who can give all their time to the planting work. It is also important to note that "simple church" or house church plants tend to be low on overhead but also low on congregational giving. As you build your budget from year one to year two, be sure to consider expenses that are limited to one-time startup costs.

3. Determine the planter's "gathering potential."

Next, it is critical to discern early on what a conservative "gathering/giving potential" number would be for your planter after three to four years of planting work. Here, the results of behavioral assessment tests will be helpful (see chapter 8 on planter selection). If the planter has gathered groups of more than 500 people in the past, you may be able to predict similar results. If not, then gauge your number on what seems realistic, based on the planter's past performance, with modest adjustments. One way to do that is to find out how many preexisting relationships the planter has in both the believing and non-believing communities in the area where he or she will work. A small number (under 100) would predict a smaller gathering potential.

Research has shown that the average attendance in church plants after three years is between seventy and one hundred adults. Sober thinking here is important, though we may all hope and pray for a large launch! Using the projected number of attenders after four years, you can predict the giving potential of the congregation when it is released on its own. To do this, take the number of employed, attending adults and multiply it by the average giving rate, which is 3 percent of local average income. Another way to calculate giving potential is to multiply the number of employed adults by $125 (3 percent of typical monthly income) and then multiply that number by 12. For example, if you have 150 adults attending and 90 have a job, multiply 90 by $125. The result: $11,250 in monthly income and an annual budget of $135,000.

4. Map long-term funding sustainability.
Having a balanced funding horizon clearly understood between the parent and the planter, as well as projecting a gathering and giving potential for the plant, allows you to discern a funding sustainability plan. If the plant is expected to generate an income of $135,000 in the fourth year, it would be foolish and unsustainable to fund it $170,000 in each of the first three years, thereby setting it up for a $35,000 shortfall in the fourth year when it is independent of the parent. It's much better to hold the total annual outside funding of the plant in the first year to no more than $135,000, its funding potential at year four, when it is self-sustaining. Whatever you feel to be your plant's giving potential in the fourth year should determine your funding maximum in the earlier years.

5. Phase out external support as internal support grows.
External funding should be applied to the plant in partnership with growing internal giving, such that the total support funding for any year is equal to what you expect the plant to generate when it is fully on its own. That will take place over a two- to four-year period for most plants, a fact that requires you to project internal giving by using the formula in principle 2,

and then subtract that number from the total budget, leaving a remainder to be supplied by outside supporters.

An Example

Here is an example of how the above five principles might be applied. To review, determining how much to fund a new start requires that you

- ❯ determine how long you want to fund the plant externally (*funding horizon*).
- ❯ estimate what it will cost annually to launch and sustain the plant (*preliminary budget*)
- ❯ estimate what the planter will be able to generate in new committed givers to the plant by the close of parent financial support (*gathering/ giving potential*).
- ❯ plan for the time frame of external support according to the gathering/ giving potential of the final year of support (*funding sustainability*).
- ❯ apply the external funding in a "graduated" way, according to attendance projections and goals (*graduated external support*).

Here's how all that might look on paper:

	Year 1	Year 2	Year 3	Year 4
Attendees with a job	20	40	60	90
Internal giving	30k	60k	90k	135k
External support	95k	65k	35k	0
Planter fundraising	10k	10k	10k	0
TOTAL	135k	135k	135k	135k

Internal giving based on $125 per month per employed attendee

This may all seem a bit complex and obtuse, and perhaps coldly calculating. But the principle is a simple one that can be understood by anyone who has been a parent. As a parent you want to give your child enough support (emotional, spiritual, and financial) to enable your child to develop and mature well, but not so much that your son or daughter develops a permanent dependence on you as a parent. It isn't always easy to live this out, but all good parents are aware of the importance of taking the time to think this through and make wise decisions. As with our children, so it is with our church plants.

This may all seem rather unspiritual as well. Don't we have to trust God to provide what we need to plant a church? Of course! But the issue here is not whether we trust in God's provision but how to steward our resources so we can plant a church that will become vigorous and self-sustaining and that will itself join the multiplication movement.

It should be said that the example we are using here is not meant to perfectly represent every context. You will likely have to modify figures to fit your context while honoring the basic principles. It is encouraging to see new cost-effective models emerging for church planting—which only broaden the options available to a parent congregation.

When to Fund?

Planting a new church requires that those involved take a leap of faith. The planter takes a risk with his or her time, family, and security, prayerfully trusting that God will bless the work with growth and success. Those who will attend the plant entrust their energy, resources, and hopes for the project as a venture of faith. The parent congregation risks many of those same elements, and high on that list is the capital resources to support the planter. Putting tens of thousands of dollars into kingdom work has always had a measure of risk. And God has called us to be both wise (Luke 16:1-12) and entrepreneurial (Matt. 25:14-30) in our kingdom investments.

So when do we accept the risk associated with funding a new plant? Here are three basic approaches:

Categorical funding: Full funding when a commitment is made to a planter

This approach to external support timing is one that makes a long-term commitment to the church planter, assuming that there will be no major violations of the shared agreement (ethics, theology, denominational distinctive). Categorical funding is a commitment to fund the plant (primarily the planter) for the full extent of the external funding phase, as negotiated by parent and planter. The plant may have a rocky season along the way, but the parent stays fully invested, keeping its commitment to funding.

The advantage of this approach is the security it gives to the planter and the recognition that there may be a slow start in internal giving during the early phase. Categorical funding assures the planter that the parent is committed to the plant and to its success. It assumes a fairly high level of risk in that commitment, knowing that if the plant is not successful the parenting church will still likely expend much, if not all, of its committed dollars.

This approach to funding is most useful when there is a high measure of trust and a well-developed sense of mutual accountability among the church planter, the parenting church, and others who are providing funding.

From Paul

When Brookside Christian Reformed Church decided to plant a church, it tapped a well-known, likeable existing member of Brookside to serve as the church planter. This person was a highly regarded recent seminary graduate who had done remarkably well, both in a church planting internship experience and in church planting assessment evaluations. Because of the trust, mutual respect, and development inherent in this relationship, categorical funding was the obvious choice and was relatively easy to obtain.

Conditional funding: Annual funding that is renewable each year
Church planting ministry requires measurements. There is little room for "simply being faithful" without showing fruitfulness. Successful church planters thrive on achieving measurable results. Conditional funding develops a contract between the planter and parent based on measurable "benchmarks" and then ties external funding to the achievement of those markers. While conditional funding should not be rigid or unbending, it does mark out clear expectations on a yearly basis (sometimes monthly or quarterly also) that are the condition for future support. This model is somewhat less risky for the parenting church, given that it can withdraw from the relationship if performance is poor. It is somewhat more risky for the planter, knowing that the parent must see results to ensure funding in the future.

Cooperative funding: Short-term external funding triggered by significant internal giving
The lowest-risk model for parent church funding is one in which the planter brings to the parent a strong group of thirty to fifty or more core group leaders who are already giving to the project but need a partner to help them employ their planter full time so they can move from a substantial core group to a sustainable ministry. Cooperative funding works because

the parent sees significant growth momentum, which builds confidence in a favorable outcome. When these relationships come together, it is often a wonderful and relatively quick experience of success and joy.

Cooperative funding opportunities may not come often to congregations eager to parent, so it is more likely that they will choose between the categorical and conditional funding models. A decision about which funding model is best for your parenting opportunity should be based on the amount of risk you're willing to accept as a parent, the trust level you have with your planter, and the circumstances you face in the parenting opportunity.

Who Will Fund?

External funding in a new church start is like a pie: the whole is made up of many slices. We have already talked about the slice of funding that comes from the internal giving of those who are committed to the core group and other attendees of the new plant. But there are many other sources that should also be considered:

- **Friends and family of the planter.** When the planter raises funds from friends and family, they form a significant accountability relationship. These people will sacrifice for their close friend, and their friend will sacrifice for them.

- **Parent church funds.** Parenting churches should remember to include church planting in their annual church budget, just as they do staff salaries, utility bills, missionary support, and so on. A pastor friend once said to me, "We fund the things that are important to us." Don't make the mistake of seeing your church planting efforts as an addition to the budget or as a luxury item that can easily be dismissed when finances get tight. Value church planting as highly as the apostle Paul did. Make it an essential part of the budget. This will inspire your congregation to keep it a priority.

- **Other partner churches.** Your church may decide not to "go it alone" when it comes to parenting. Partnering with other churches is a good way to share the financial load.

- **Denominational agencies.** Ecclesiastical accountability and support are important for new church pastors as they live on the outer boundaries of their church communities. The denomination needs them for mission, and they need the denomination. Local, regional, and national bodies are often able to provide support.

◑ **Microenterprise or tent-making.** These efforts are often wonderful means to widen the network of relationships for the planter and thus are pathways for gospel conversations. One example of this is opening a neighborhood coffee house that helps fund a church plant as it builds relationships. It is also important to be realistic and to recognize that a low-paying job that does not help the planter network with large numbers of people is likely to be a long-term liability to the planter and plant. Bi-vocational work is best when it augments the planter's objectives with both finances and additional networks.

The parent congregation is not the only source of funding for the new plant, nor should it be. When others are "in the game" there is added value at many levels, both tangible and spiritual. Helping the planter develop those connections is an important role you can play.

A parent church (or another partner church) can also support the plant beyond actual dollars given. For example, the infrastructure costs of a church plant can be notably reduced if the parent church provides office space to the planter, free use of its facilities for ministry needs, use of office equipment and technology (copiers, computers), bookkeeping resources, and so on. While these arrangements are not cost-free and are not meant to continue indefinitely, they can be extremely helpful in the early months or years of the church plant. In some cases the actual financial costs to the parent church are minimal, while the savings to the church plant are substantial.

The right planter often will be able to tap into resources simply because he or she has established a high level of trust with the established church. One study revealed that "63 percent of planters of fast-growing churches were personally involved in raising additional funds beyond what the sponsoring agency provided" (Stephen Gray, *Planting Fast-growing Churches*, p. 72). This trust will encourage some longtime members of a parenting church to increase their total giving so as to continue to financially support the parent congregation while also giving "new" funds to the church planter.

Setting Your Planter Up for Funding Success

Often, the best people to make the case for funding a new plant are the planters themselves. Others can and should advocate, but the planter is the prime visionary of the new start and thus the best communicator. Setup the planter for success by helping him or her engage with donor prospects at every opportunity. Together you can develop the funding base the new church will need for success.

Stephen Gray found that when planters are significantly involved in raising funds, the plant is more likely to be stronger and larger. If a prospective planter does not want to raise funds, that should sound a "caution" alarm to your hiring team. The ability to sell people on a planting vision is the first success or failure of a church plant. It is best to involve the planter in every dimension of the fund development process, from designing the campaign to making the calls. In some situations where the denomination and the parent church have a large investment, we suggest that the planter raise 10 to 30 percent of the outside funding from friends and family. To accomplish that goal you need to set up your planter for funding success.

From Paul

At Brookside Christian Reformed Church we gave our new church planter a "Fishing License" within our congregation and network. This meant that he had full permission, and even encouragement, to seek out funding within our "pond." This fishing license was public knowledge, and we were not bashful in talking about it. It was especially important for me, as senior pastor, to encourage people to financially embrace this new enterprise as one of our own.

We learned this lesson the hard way. Years ago we were tangentially involved in a church plant started by our local judicatory. We were asked to be the "calling" church for the church planter, I was involved in some mentoring of the planter, and we even had a few members become part of the initial core group of the plant. But we never really saw ourselves as parents and never fully invested ourselves. There was no fishing license granted to the new planter (or even considered), and soon the fledgling church floundered and failed. Although we gave a few "fish" to the new plant, we never gave them a fishing license and certainly didn't help them learn how to fish.

Stewardship development is key work in both the pre-launch and the post-launch phase of the ministry. Raising startup funds is necessary for allowing the planter to be devoted to the work full time, which is the optimal pattern.

Developing a stewardship culture in the hearts and minds of those attending both the parenting church and the new church plant is critical to the long-term sustainability of the plant. Again, research shows that plants that teach biblical stewardship within the first six months of their existence are more likely to thrive and demonstrate greater health than those who avoid it. The problem is that most church planters are not comfortable doing so. For that reason significant training is important. Sometimes church planting boot-camp experiences will include this training. If not, we urge you to encourage growth in the following key areas of stewardship leadership:

- ❍ **Biblical and theological foundations of stewardship development.** Too often planters view money merely as a commodity needed for them to do their work. This mentality will severely dampen their energy, creativity, and confidence in developing donors. Biblical stewardship is a key area the planter must master if the ministry is to thrive.
- ❍ **Strategic planning.** Because people are more likely to give to the future, as opposed to past debt, it is critical that planters have a solid grasp of the strategic planning for their ministry goals and are able to cast a compelling vision for donors.
- ❍ **Communicating ministry vision.** Using words and images skillfully to cultivate ministry vision is key. It is invaluable at the earliest stages of a plant to develop a case for support and to practice telling a story of the vision that will appeal to donors.
- ❍ **Ministry worthiness.** Earning the right to receive a gift requires transparency, accountability, and maturity. If planters expect people to give generously to the new start, they must show that they can be trusted with the gifts people give.
- ❍ **Training.** Unfortunately, most seminaries do not provide the necessary level of practical stewardship training for planters and pastors. You may need to seek out a training provider, but your insistence that the planter be trained is a major factor in future success.

Developing a sustainable funding plan is a significant part of successful parenting. Any time you invest here, in partnership with your planter whenever possible, will help build a stronger foundation.

Next Step Questions

1. Have you determined the three- to four-year gathering potential of your planter? From this number, have you gained clarity (using the formulas offered in this chapter) on how much outside funding you will need to cover the launch phase? Does your funding plan set up the plant for sustainability?

2. What is your preliminary budget for the plant for year 1 and year 2? Have you built "one-time" costs into the first year?

3. Which funding strategy will you pursue as relates to "risk management": categorical, conditional, or cooperative?

4. How can you help your planter be most successful in raising funds? Have you accessed all of the potential funding partners for your project?

5. Are you reasonably confident that you are neither underfunding nor overfunding your new plant?

Chapter 6

Discerning a Planting Opportunity

"If opportunity isn't knocking, build a door." —*Milton Berle*

Recently a pastor friend reported to me that the church's ministry board, which had been cool and unreceptive to church planting, had suddenly become excited by the prospect of being a church-planting church. Its members had become aware of a newly arriving group of Christian refugees from Southeast Asia looking for a place to worship, and the board offered their building. Today they are well on their way to parenting this new community toward sustainability. The lesson here is that sometimes opportunities to parent come looking for us. At other times we are the ones who need to do the seeking and exploring.

There was a time when church planting opportunities were discerned only "horizontally." We unfolded city or county maps and plotted new start opportunities based on where new construction was happening. While that method is still useful, another approach has become prominent. The "vertical" approach gives us new eyes to see the many ethnic and generational layers that exist in one community, and the many different types of churches that could serve that community. This added dimension, together with an overall shortage of new churches, provides many opportunities for qualified church planters and sponsoring parent congregations.

Today's increasing cultural diversity challenges us to look beyond first impressions when we consider a community for church planting. Our cities and counties now include people groups that are underserved and sometimes unrecognized. We used to refer to "unreached people groups" only in terms of world missions, but in our global society unreached people groups exist all around us. As we plant churches in North America we need to be aware of the micro-cultures that exist in our communities, as well as of their unique generational, language, ethnic, and socioeconomic features.

Each of our local churches also has unique socioeconomic features. While all churches can and should strive to reflect the diversity of God's kingdom, no individual church will be able to effectively reach and minister to all groups. Moreover, every local church makes certain judgments about worship style and ministry focus. Those judgments define who they are and who they can reach. A parent church that recognizes and owns its own cultural, ministry, worship, and socioeconomic realties will best be able to extend its reach and ministry by planting a new church that looks different, feels different, and reaches different people. The point is to be open to the possibilities that God may place before us and recognize what we bring to the experience.

With greater awareness of diversity, we can see that there are multiple planting options in our communities. These exciting changes are igniting new visions for church planting all over North America. Having said this, it is wise to take the time for a deep study of your context. This step in the process is rarely wasted energy, as the results can be used in many ways, from developing a ministry plan to confirming a planter match to appealing to donors. At the very least, this study will give you a rich insight into the mission field that you are in.

A First Look at Opportunity

How many churches can your community reasonably sustain? "Saturation church planting" is an expression used to refer to the number of healthy churches a city or community could or should have. Saturation church planting involves planting enough churches to serve the diversity, as well as the size, of your community.

Experts suggest that there should be one healthy church for every 1,000 people in a community. If we accept the fact that average weekly church attendance hovers around 17 percent (see chapter 2 and the research of Dave Olson), that would mean that a community should be able to see at least one healthy and vital church of 170 people for every 1,000 people in that community.

A first look at opportunity in your community would be to simply take current population data for an area and look at the number of healthy churches in that same area. That ratio should be an indicator of how underserved the community is. Of course this method does not take into consideration an effort to reach beyond the 17 percent average church attendance, which new church plants can do when they focus on the needs of particular segments of the population.

Community Church Need Calculator

It may take some digging to find the relevant information you need to make this calculation, and if your community is large it will take time, but the result will be eye-opening.

- ◗ Contact your chamber of commerce and determine the estimated population 3-5 years from the date you propose to begin planting. Divide that number by 1000.
- ◗ Determine the total number of churches in your community either online or through your local yellow pages.
- ◗ Make a conservative estimation of the number of churches in significant decline (consider churches with no full time pastor, no longer a match to their context, over 20 years old or under 50 attendees).
- ◗ Subtract line #3 from line #2. This should give you the total number of healthy churches in your community.
- ◗ Subtract line #4 from line #1 to find the potential number of new churches in your community.

Most communities provide multiple opportunities to plant churches, especially when underserved populations are in the equation. Hopefully the opportunity is close enough in both physical and cultural/social terms so that your people can become actively involved as core team participants and supporters of the planter. Sometimes, however, the opportunity is physically close but culturally and socially distant. This situation requires some deeper thinking and planning. Mid-urban communities (those zones between the urban and suburban areas) are often the place where rapid social change is taking place. These communities often have more affordable homes for people in transition and others who find suburban or gentrified urban spaces unaffordable. The social mobility experience in these mid-urban spaces creates great opportunity for new church starts.

Opportunity and Diversity

The face of North America is rapidly changing. In 2008 the U.S. Census reported that roughly one-third of the population represented minority groups. That diverse minority is projected to become the diverse majority by the year 2042. As striking as that projection is, an even more arresting statistic confronts us. In the year 1900 Europe and North America were home to more than 80 percent of the world's known Christian community. Today that number is closer to 40 percent and declining fast. Increasingly, the face of global Christianity is African, Asian, and Hispanic. So the trend toward cultural diversity in North America impacts the church before it impacts the general population, primarily because so many immigrants are Christians. This amazing confluence of trends gives us opportunities unforeseen in times past.

The opening story in this chapter paints a very real picture of the impact of the macro-trend that immigration is presenting today. Immigrant people are seeking places to worship, and existing churches sometimes have more space than they need. Parenting can be as simple as the bold hospitality of welcoming the stranger among us and making a space for a new worshipping community. A historically Dutch community near my home has seen a remarkable rise in its Hispanic population, yet only a very few church plants are focused on that opportunity.

Cultural Distance and the 60 Percent

The more we begin to look at opportunities to plant new churches in North America, the more we face issues of strategy and resources. The vast majority of our resources and energy for gospel witness in North America lies within a relatively small sector of the population. Alan Hirsch, writing from the perspective of his home in Australia, describes the problem: "In Australia we have the somewhat farcical situation of 95 percent of evangelical churches tussling with each other to reach 12 percent of the population. And this becomes a significant missional problem because it raises the question, 'What about the vast majority of the population [in Australia's case, 85 percent; in the United States, about 65 percent] that report alienation from *precisely* that form of church?'" (*The Forgotten Ways*, Brazos Press, 2006. pp. 36-37). Hirsch exposes the American church's preference for going after, and nearly fighting for, the 40 percent of the wider population that already has "cultural proximity" to the church and her message, while nearly ignoring the 60 percent or more that do not.

Hirsch has adapted a measurement from the world of missiology to map the issue of cultural distance and gospel engagement. He calls it the "M-scale." In this scale "m" indicates "one significant cultural barrier to the meaningful communication of the gospel," such as language, history, religion, worldview, culture, and so on.

The M-scale is a continuum that can be graphed like this:

M0------------M1------------M2-----------M3-----------M4

Here is the key that Hirsch provides:

M0-M1: Those with some concept of Christianity who speak the same language, have similar interests, are probably of the same nationality, and are from a class grouping similar to yours or your church's. Most of your friends would probably fit into this bracket.

M1-M2: Here we go to the average non-Christian in our context: a person who has little real awareness of, or interest in, Christianity but is suspicious of the church (they have heard bad things). These people might be politically correct, socially aware, and open to spirituality. This category might also include those previously offended by a bad experience of church or Christians.

M2-M3: People in this group have absolutely no idea about Christianity. They might be part of an ethnic group with different religious impulses. . . . This group will definitely include people actively antagonistic toward Christianity as they understand it.

M3-M4: This group might be inhabited by ethnic and religious groupings like Muslims or Jews. The fact that they are in the West might ameliorate some of the distance, but just about everything else gets in the way of a meaningful dialogue. They are highly resistant to the gospel.

—from *The Forgotten Ways*, Brazos Press, 2006, p. 57.

Hirsch's focus on the 60 percent calls attention to our avoidance of those who would likely fall into the M3 and M4 categories.

Some years ago I preached from time to time at a "drive-in church." Granted, the worship music and format were fairly traditional, by North American standards. However, I soon became aware of the wide swath of people who are very uncomfortable with crowds and public places, to the point that they will not attend a typical church. They would likely be M2-M3 people. They desire more than a TV preacher on Sunday mornings but cannot bear to enter an actual place of worship for all sorts of reasons. So they come to the drive-in church—in significant numbers! Others cannot relate to our music or are turned off by "evangelical politics" or feel alienated by our socioeconomic standard of living or to what they perceive as our intolerance.

I am currently rejoicing in the unfolding of a new church plant in our region that focuses on individuals and families impacted by the experience of autism and its related spectrum. These people have often suffered greatly because of the intolerance or inability of society, including the church, to provide a place for their healing, hope, and encouragement. Because of the profound disruption that caring for their loved one has created, they feel they do not fit in anywhere and struggle in isolation. Today there is hope in new efforts by parent congregations to envision and to develop churches for these families and individuals. This is an example of a portion of the 60 percent being reached in a new way.

Hirsch goes on to cite language from the business community that differentiates between the "Red Ocean" and the "Blue Ocean." The Red Ocean is a highly competitive space in which we outmaneuver one another to reach those who shift their affiliations based on the latest appeal. The Red Ocean is the zone of the 40 percent. The Blue Ocean is the vast, uncontested market where innovation and creativity give rise to new opportunity. Hirsch is fond of the simple church movement as a way of penetrating the 60 percent. Others have focused on specialized ministries to those with emotional or physical needs. Still others have looked into vocational niches, such as a new church that exists in the artistic world of the theater district in a college community or another that has a special emphasis on eating sustainable and local foods.

Ironically, many churches today, even those that are usually viewed as healthy and vibrant, reach mostly M1 and a few M2 folks, rarely venturing out of the competitive 40 percent.

From Paul

As the pastor of Brookside Christian Reformed Church, my judgment is that we are mostly an M1, M2, and Red Ocean congregation, only beginning to make inroads into the Blue Ocean of M3. As Brookside's pastor I know that we have work to do and some rich possibilities that we are just beginning to tap. But while we continue to work and grow as a congregation, we have also launched a church plant that intentionally spends a little more time in the Blue Ocean and is reaching beyond M2 into the M3 territory. In some ways, these are only small movements, and that is precisely why I mention them. All churches can make small movements in the right direction and so make a big impact.

Of course, there is no sin in reaching those near and similar to you—the 40 percent. This is especially true if your M1 community is underchurched. Your decision to reach beyond the 40 percent should not be driven by guilt or forced obligation. Bloom where you are planted and where God opens the doors. However, in the story of the Good Samaritan Jesus called us all to reach out with acts of mercy to those who are physically close but culturally distant, setting the bar high for our ministry in the world. The invitation is to reach beyond our comfort level in mission, while recognizing that apart from a key leader and some remarkable circumstances we are limited in how far we can stretch in planting a new church. So if God has shown you an opportunity to plant a new church in a neighborhood similar to your own among people similar to your own, do not resist. But remain open and supportive of those efforts to reach the 60 percent.

The Unchurched and the Dechurched

Another way to think about your target group is by their prior experience with church. One tool to help discern this is the Engel Scale, which outlines a series of developmental steps a person might take on the way to being a fully engaged disciple of Jesus Christ. It can help us distinguish between the "unchurched" and the "dechurched." While most faith journeys are not quite as linear and predicable as we may think (many have observed rightly that for postmoderns a form of conversion to Christian community usually precedes a conversion to Christ), James Engel has given us a starting point to think about the process.

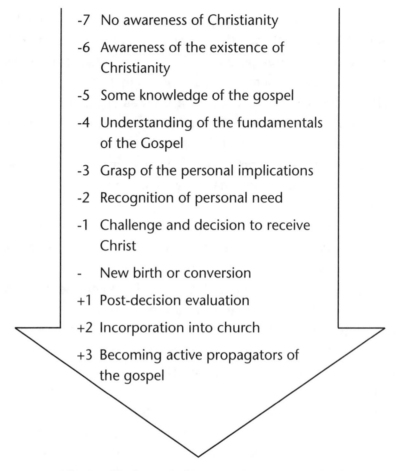

-7 No awareness of Christianity

-6 Awareness of the existence of Christianity

-5 Some knowledge of the gospel

-4 Understanding of the fundamentals of the Gospel

-3 Grasp of the personal implications

-2 Recognition of personal need

-1 Challenge and decision to receive Christ

-   New birth or conversion

+1 Post-decision evaluation

+2 Incorporation into church

+3 Becoming active propagators of the gospel

(The Engel Scale, as cited in *Perspectives on the World Christian Movement*, Ralph Winter and Steven Hawthorne, eds., William Carey Library, 1981, p. 591)

Strategies for planting a new church among the unchurched (those who are likely beginning their journey at level -6 or -7) are significantly different from those aimed at dechurched persons (who likely are at a -5 or above). Unchurched individuals are often reasonably open to forms of worship and environments that are somewhat or very traditional. They also will probably stand in need of more grounding in the stories and language of faith and the Bible. Dechurched people may be more likely to seek out an expression of church that is a reaction against the church of their youth or of the former generation. The Engel Scale can help us discern where on the pathway toward Christ those we are seeking to reach may be, and thereby the kind of plant we will seek to launch.

Developing a Target Profile

I am not fond of the word "target." It conjures up clever marketing methods that are not productive in the long run. I use it here to make the simple point that without a focused ministry objective it is difficult to make a wise leadership selection or launch plan. Trying to reach everyone in general is a great way to reach no one in particular. That does not rule out a church plant that seeks to be intentionally diverse. My experience is that even those ministries that are wonderfully diverse ethnically do, if they are well led, have a clear target. They can describe who it is they are seeking to reach. It could be a geographic target area or a particular human need, as illustrated earlier in this chapter. Most new churches today grow as specialty stores, not as shopping malls. Program diversity grows over time as they mature and blossom.

From Paul

One church I know sometimes advertises itself as a church for those "who don't like church." They are intentionally trying to target a specific subset of people who do not care for traditional worship and have great skepticism toward common church experiences. On the other hand, I sometimes like to quip that my church is "church for those who like church." These churches are not in competition with one another; rather, they are two congregations attempting to reach two entirely different targets. We can see each other as colleagues and partners, specifically because we have thought about our target focus.

Because of the season of great opportunity God has given us, developing a target focus is likely to result in several possible plant opportunities. Be prepared! Following are some steps to take as you work toward discernment.

Do a demographic study. Start with the free providers, such as city-data. com and factfinder.census.gov, and then look into those that charge a modest fee, such as Percept (perceptgroup.com) and Missioninsite (missioninsite.

com). Each of these providers will give you a great start in reading your community. Many of these providers will do more than offer numbers. They may help you identify "psychographic" information, which includes family and interest types. Often a denominational leader can help you leverage these tools. Another source, peoplegroups.info, is a good way to discover underserved people near you.

Interview area planters. These people are likely to have insights about the underserved people in your community. In many cases they have already come to recognize that their plant cannot reach everyone and may even be willing to partner with you if you can agree on a similar target.

Get out into the community and listen. Using the results of the demographic study and other input, interview people who live and work in the community to discern what the needs are. One project I am currently working on is hiring local people to do a community survey to discern needs and openness to a new church plant. Using non-church people to do community surveys is a good way to elicit an honest response.

Discern the spiritual climate and movement of the Holy Spirit. Prayer walking is a great way to begin to see what God sees. Ask the Lord for insight into the places where the gospel message is most needed. Seek to sense where God is already at work and on the move. Ask the Lord for local "people of peace" to be partners in your efforts.

List and prioritize the potential new church plants. How many different underserved people groups can you identify? Build a list to share with other mission-minded people. Can any of these be reasonably "doubled up"? Refine your list and then prioritize based on the leadership God is bringing you for a core team or lead planter. If you have not selected the lead planter, you will probably not want to firm up your decision yet.

Ask your lead planter. If you have selected a leader, that person is probably already oriented toward a particular group of people. Be sure you make his or her input a top priority. This factor deserves some special consideration.

The Priority of Planter Preference

It is important that we take a moment to issue a caution here. Often a committee or team can become so deeply engaged in the work of target discernment that they "over-invent" the church plant. While their efforts are well-intentioned, the team can develop detailed plans and programs with the idea that they can just "plug in" a planter to their ministry project. This removes the planter from the foundational planning, setting up potential collisions down the road. Selecting and confirming a "target community" to be reached is important work, but it needs to be held loosely and confirmed through your planter selection process. It is likely that the right planter will already have evidence of effective impact within a similar target group to the one you are considering for your new ministry.

Remember that the only person truly qualified to plant the church God is prompting you to parent is a leader who is able to think clearly and in detail about how to do it and is passionately invested in it. Read that sentence twice! Your lead planter should be open to input, but he or she also needs to have the freedom to shape and design the plant. This issue ties in to a wider issue of church plant leadership and oversight. The key principles to honor are these:

- ❷ The planter should have freedom to develop the ministry within agreed-upon boundaries. Micromanaging is not a healthy relationship between parent and planter.
- ❷ Outlining a potential target and general launch plan in pencil and later negotiating a refinement between the planter and the parent leadership is appropriate. The first step is best done before the planter is hired.

The broader issues of planter freedom and accountability will be addressed in chapter 9. For our purpose here, be sure there is agreement from the start between parent and planter as to the target.

This Is God's Mission

It is of paramount importance in church planting that we maintain the centrality of God as the prime missionary, the church planter already at work. When we do good discernment work we discover where God is already developing receptivity to the gospel. If we remember that, our efforts will not be forced but will flow in the power of the Holy Spirit.

Earlier in this chapter we referenced a new plant directed toward "the 60 percent," in this case specifically targeting individuals and families with members on the autism spectrum. In the unfolding of this particular project I sense the remarkable presence of the Lord as people step up and resources open up and community interest rises up. Yes, there is a great need, but that is exactly where we might expect Jesus to show up! When I first met with the lead pastor of the parent church I was excited by his vision to develop these unique churches all across North America in response to the spike in diagnoses of autism. But even in our enthusiasm we stopped to pray, leaning deeply into God and seeking his direction. Identifying a target audience is only an exercise in marketing strategy if God is not part of your mission.

Look for indications of God's work. These might include

- **People of peace.** These people are not necessarily believers but are supportive of your presence and efforts. They could be business leaders, community leaders, or neighbors.
- **Spiritual and human brokenness.** In Jesus' words, "Blessed are the poor in spirit," and in other Scriptures we hear God's inclination toward those who are in great need.
- **Spiritual revival/awakening.** Look for people or churches experiencing genuine repentance and a turning back to their communities in mission and witness.
- **Grassroots discipleship.** Look for small networks of believers that form in anticipation of a wider ministry vision. Jesus called us to make disciples and baptize—to do individual and corporate ministry.
- **Miraculous acts of God.** Conversions, healings, and restoration are signs of God's mission to reconcile the world to himself and of God's missionary advance.
- **Planters seeking a sending and support agency.** You may be surprised to find people who are already feeling called by God to reach the very area you are being directed toward. One way to find those individuals is to network with other church planters near you.
- **Confirmation from other believers.** If God is speaking to you, he is certainly able and likely to speak to others as well. Who else might be able to confirm your direction?

Not every setting is fertile ground for the gospel. We know that from Jesus' parable of the soils (Luke 8). Seeking to discern the receptivity of the soil and the work of the Holy Spirit is important in this phase of a multiplication move.

Next Step Questions

1. What is the church-to-population ratio in the community you are exploring for a plant? What tools should you use to gain insight into the features of your desired area?

2. Are there opportunities in M1, M2, M3, or M4 segments of your community that you should consider? Using the "Blue Ocean" analogy, what underserved groups could your planter consider?

3. Using the tools listed in this chapter, build a list of potential target profiles. How would you describe each profile as a preliminary target?

4. What input has your planter given you as an indicator of his or her target passion?

5. Where is God at work? What indicators of receptivity suggest the moving of the Holy Spirit?

Chapter 7

Selecting the Right Parenting Model

"A hunch is creativity trying to tell you something." —*Frank Capra*

When I meet with Roger and his friends, I just know I am in for a conversation that will stretch my thinking. Roger is a church planter who has seen his plant's efforts blessed to such a degree that now, five years after its inception, the new church is exploring the launch of a new church plant themselves. Roger has a passion for true multiplication: churches planting churches, and those churches planting more. He itches to see Paul's vision in 2 Timothy 2:2 happen: "The things you have heard me say in the presence of many witnesses entrust to reliable people who will also be qualified to teach others." In that simple verse there are four gospel generations: the gospel communicated to Paul, to Timothy, to "reliable people," and to "others." When I talk with Roger I get excited to see that third gospel transmission taking place in a multiplication movement!

But if the transmission is to occur, it needs new forms and structures. For example, while the parent church of Roger's congregation planted one model of church, the new plant (Roger's ministry) will usually daughter in a significantly different way. That may be due to issues of resources and of style. This is exactly what Roger and his friends were dealing with as I met with them. Each person in the room represented a young church plant that wanted to multiply. Each, however, was faced with a very different set of initial circumstances than those they experienced themselves as a plant. So the creative types were in their element! Some planned to go with a multisite model as a way of keeping costs down. Others were exploring simple or house church models as a way to accelerate multiplication. Each was focused on reaching new people and raising up new leaders, unimpeded by the barriers that challenged them.

Church planting is not a "cookie cutter" endeavor. Every opportunity, planter, target community, launch plan, and resource strategy is a "custom job." I am in debt to my good friend and national Reformed Church in America leader Tim Vink, who has captured a listing of possible multiplication models and their advantages and disadvantages. Following are sixteen different ways a congregation can make a multiplication move. Scan the list and you are likely to have a whole new surge of creative ideas for your context—and you might come up with a seventeenth or eighteenth way!

Sixteen Ways to Parent

1. Parachute. Send a planter and his or her family into a new community to start from scratch, without the advantage of a parent congregation. This is a "missionary strategy" of church planting because the church planter has no previous connection with the community. The church planter must learn the community's history and culture and use an appropriate form of evangelism that speaks to the needs of the people living in the area. The parachute model is typically used by a parent church in a city or an area with significant population growth but no proximal parent. For example, several denominations in the suburbs of Phoenix used this model as the population exploded by 97 percent from the late 1990s to the mid-2000s.

> ❿ *Advantages:* You can start anywhere the Spirit leads you, and you can extend the church's reach to new territory or people groups.
> ❿ *Disadvantages:* This is usually more expensive—up to $100,000 annually—and has a lower success rate: 25-50 percent. It also takes a highly motivated and gifted individual to lead the plant because the church planter and his or her family have no immediate support group. They are truly missionaries, attempting to create a core group of families to plant the church from scratch.

2. Team Migration. Instead of a single family moving into a new area, team migration involves an entire group of Christian leaders and members of a church purposefully relocating their families simultaneously to a new community to plant a church. This was done dramatically a few years ago by a dozen families in the Detroit-area church of a friend of mine. They went through an assessment process to determine their gifts and then moved their families to Salt Lake City to plant a church. I have also seen this done in California, where a parent church encouraged its members to move into a new neighborhood in order to plant a church in a part of the city that was being resettled by a new people group. The members sold their homes and moved into the new area. Typically, in a team migration the team averages between five and thirty people, just enough to form a solid core group.

> *Advantages:* Starting from a much stronger base gives this method a higher success rate. Christian community and multi-gifted leaders are already intact, and a base of emotional and financial support is jump-started.
> *Disadvantages:* It's hard to find this level of freedom and commitment in a group. Uprooting and moving also means developing new relationships in a new place.

3. Hive Off. A large congregation of 300 or more hires a planter to come on staff for nine months or so—enough time to gather a healthy group with which to plant a new church, usually in the same community. This group can range in size from thirty to more than two hundred. In Princeton, New Jersey, a pastor explained to me how his denomination had encouraged its pastors to hire church planters. These people would eventually invite members of the congregation to join them in planting a new congregation relatively close to the first church but in a new area of the city. This way the members of the older congregation would not need to travel a great distance in order to attend the new church plant. A few of the members from the first church would then leave and join the new plant. Eventually, when the new church got large enough, it would plant another new church that was relatively close but in a new neighborhood or a new part of the city.

Wooddale Church in Minneapolis, of which Leith Anderson is the senior pastor, has planted nine churches using this model. Wooddale gives permission to its church planters to engage in what they call "open season" on the congregation. This means that the church planter can approach any church member or staff person to ask that person to join the new church plant.

I could cite many examples in which a parenting church gave away its best leaders, its best musicians, its best teachers, and its best givers to a new church plant because the planter recruited them. One might think that this would devastate the parent church, but God honored the missional commitment by providing for new leadership within the parent church. Humanly speaking, this happened in part because room was made for other members to exercise gifts they were not fully using.

> *Advantages:* Called and motivated members will go with the planter. Since a strong functioning body is sent out, the new plant will

typically become self-supporting and self-governing in a short time, often eighteen months or less. This method also establishes strong ties between parent and daughter churches.

- ◑ *Disadvantages:* The parent church has a larger "rebuilding" process, although God seems to supply many new members to the parent church in the process of this vision being lived out.

4. Satellite. A congregation is started at another location in the same area as its parent church and remains under the leadership of the parent church staff and governing board. This form is becoming increasingly popular with larger congregations that have a strong "brand" in the community and a growing desire to multiply. Some of these satellite congregations are video venues, where the music is live but the Sunday sermon is a rebroadcast of the prior Sunday or Saturday evening's service. In others, the service is conducted by live feed from the parent church. In still others, there is an onsite preacher who develops that local congregation.

- ◑ *Advantages:* This method is often better at targeting, with a new location or style, an underserved group for which the parent church has a heart. It covers leadership and administration needs centrally and has low costs.
- ◑ *Disadvantages:* The new church can remain dependent on the central church longer or be over-controlled. It can also foster a "one-preacher phenomenon," in which new communicators are not developed or given opportunity to use their gifts.

5. Multisite to Planting. An existing church opens several new venues or locations to reach the unchurched, often using video messages from the parent church and live worship and ministry teams in the secondary locations. Some churches have up to twenty-two services a weekend this way. New members are initially added to the parent church, but in time some of these sites "spin off" as self-governing, self-sustaining congregations when they are further developed in leadership, body life, finances, and supporting structures.

- ◑ *Advantages:* This hybrid of expanding the parent church and reaching creatively into the community allows a gradual and tested timeline for planting. Parent churches have a strong sense of ownership in the planting process.

❯ *Disadvantages:* This model can require extensive technological expertise and a dynamic communicator from the parent church staff.

6. Adoption. A struggling established church comes under the supportive relationship of another local church and classis, or other regional judicatory, to promote greater growth and mutual benefit. In Phoenix, an older RCA congregation that was struggling "adopted" a newer non-denominational congregation. The newer congregation was more culturally diverse and better reflected the multicultural nature of the surrounding neighborhood, which had undergone tremendous change over the past few years. This diversity greatly benefited the older congregation, and the two congregations eventually merged into one united RCA congregation.

❯ *Advantages:* The adopted church is more developed and can grow rapidly with new partnering relationships. This can often bring diversity to the denomination while demonstrating kingdom unity.

❯ *Disadvantages:* The new church comes with its own history and leadership, so it will assimilate more slowly in classis relationships. These churches may need to consider a non-seminary-trained pastor, since not all leaders of adoptive churches are M.Div. graduates.

7. House Church Network. As more and more people in our postmodern era question the value of institutionalized religion, the model of house churches is taking hold. These small communities often appeal to people who are "allergic" to large institutions, including churches. These communities are poised to be more missional by encouraging their members to engage their neighbors in spiritual conversations similar to the way missionaries do in an overseas mission field. These new "missionaries" invite their neighbors into their homes for Bible study, prayer, and fellowship. Smaller, multiplying home churches reach the unchurched and disciple new believers in daily community. Doesn't this sound like Acts 2? Typically these groups are made up of five to fifteen people, with 90-100 percent of worship, fellowship, discipleship, ministry, and mission occurring in the homes and neighborhoods. Sometimes these house churches network together like parents of home-schooled children do when they bring their children together for a field trip, a sport, or a social event. One house church pastor I know says that his house church is intentional about reaching the people who live on their block and in the surrounding neighborhood.

❂ *Advantages:* House churches are very inexpensive but have high participation from the people involved. These churches can "travel" and reproduce anywhere, using elder leadership and readily equipping new leadership. This method has a deeper discipleship impact than the typical congregational model and is based far more on "go and make disciples" than on "come to church to visit us."

❂ *Disadvantages:* Churches can remain small and independent if they aren't well led by visionary and evangelistic leaders. This method requires some unlearning of typical church processes and expectations in favor of small group dynamics, and it's harder for these groups to connect to typical denominational structures.

8. Cell-Celebration Model. A planter originates the new church by developing multiple neighborhood cell groups. These groups move from monthly private worship with one to four cells to weekly private worship of five to eight cells to weekly public worship of nine or more cells. The cells carry 50 to 75 percent of the worship, fellowship, discipleship, ministry, and mission of the church. This is a middle-ground approach between a house church and a typical "congregational model."

❂ *Advantages:* This model bridges the gap between many people's current expectations about how to "do" church and the effective church model from the early church, which is closer to today's simple but expanding house church network model. This model is better than most others at encouraging deep discipleship.

❂ *Disadvantages:* It's hard work to develop effective cell groups that multiply believers, leaders, and new cells, and it can be challenging to figure out how to minister to the children in the cell groups.

9. Host Campus. A larger church with good facilities offers space and encouragement to a start-up church. The start-up church has little ministry supervision from the host and is often predominantly of another ethnic group or economic class. This is also called "nesting."

New Hope Community Church hosts a Korean-speaking congregation in its facility, has planted a Spanish-speaking congregation, and is starting another English-speaking congregation to reach young married couples who live in the community. With two Sunday-morning English-speaking services, this means that there are five worship services in the church's facilities. What makes this work is a spirit of hospitality and a vision for God's greater kingdom that is shared by all four congregations. As Jim Poit says, "There is a great desire on everyone's part to see the other congregations succeed. Fundamentally we do not see each other as separate entities, but rather as one body with a common purpose: to reach our community for Christ."

> ❯ *Advantages:* If the host church offers facilities at low or no rent, this is a tremendous financial help to the newer church. It also maximizes the use of existing facilities.
> ❯ *Disadvantages:* Tensions can arise if there are significant cultural differences or a weak relationship between the churches. The relationship can become abusive if the host church raises the rent or the guest church becomes unruly.

10. Sponsoring Church. A parent church plants a new family of faith on its campus until growth allows the daughter church to move out on its own. This kind of church incubator intentionally involves a much higher investment on the part of the parent church, often involving the coaching of the planter and supervision of the new ministry's direction and development.

> ❯ *Advantages:* This model has the same advantages as the host campus model (see model 9, above). It also provides a stronger start for the new church, has a higher success rate, involves less conflict, and lowers the temptation for either church to abuse the situation. It may not require the parent church to give any members to the plant.
> ❯ *Disadvantages:* This model requires purposeful leadership on the part of the parent church, along with wisdom and skill to coach and empower the new church, making the relationship mutually beneficial. Tips: Implement a coordinating committee with members from both churches to help ensure fairness in scheduling and cost sharing, and consider holding joint services two to four times a year to keep communication open and celebrate one another's successes.

11. Church Split. Agenda disharmony or a leadership crisis precipitates the rapid departure of a specific group of people, who then form a new congregation nearby. While this is not ideal, it does happen, and it can become redemptive in the long run.

> ❯ *Advantages:* People have sufficient motivation to take a risk and plant a new church after enough pressure and heartache builds up in a

"non-reproducing" environment. The energy of the situation often means the new church will survive.

> ● *Disadvantages:* In a church split there is plenty of pain and blame to go around, and the witness of both churches is hurt. If the new congregation is caught up in the painful past and doesn't develop a clear new vision for ministry and outreach, it will have difficulty growing.

12. Repotting. A new congregation starts meeting in an available building after a former church closes. The typical scenario goes like this: a community changes socially, economically, culturally, or ethnically, and the local established congregation is no longer able to serve the community's needs. So the church reaches the end of its lifecycle and, often in the midst of great discouragement and disillusionment, the church board decides to close the doors, convinced that no form of ministry is possible in that place.

Then a new congregation comes along, either buys or rents the facility, and grows a wonderful ministry there. Why does the new congregation grow when the older one couldn't? For some, it's the "spark" of a new leader who connects at a deeper level with the local community. Also, when a new congregation is repotted in place of an older and dying one, the new church is not hampered by tradition or structures and can easily change its course to meet the spiritual needs of the local community. One note: it is crucial that the new church have a distinct new name and identity.

> ● *Advantages:* A fresh start is often more effective than attempting to revitalize an older congregation. In terms of reaching the unchurched and ministering to the community, repotting can provide a legacy opportunity for a declining church, whose closing may end up benefiting the kingdom.
> ● *Disadvantages:* This model does not increase the number of churches in the community. It can also be difficult for members of the former church to accept unless enough celebration and closure take place.

13. Relaunch/Fresh Start. An existing, struggling church recognizes that a dramatic change is needed and that the existing team has been unable to build a sustainable, healthy ministry. A relaunch requires that the members of the existing leadership team resign and the ministry "goes dark" for a while. A new leadership team is developed, along with a new vision and new strategies. A seasoned coach and oversight team are needed to guide the process, which involves a host of emotional and strategic challenges.

- *Advantages:* In this model, a committed core group re-imagines ministry and mission while there is still a critical mass of attendees. This often creates a chance to solve deep problems.
- *Disadvantages:* A relaunch takes courageous leadership and coaching, along with skilled assessment of the place and people of the replanting, to avoid the "same song, second verse" phenomenon.

14. Turnaround Church. A declining church of fifty or fewer members is revitalized with new leadership and vision in such a way that a whole new congregation is birthed. This often includes a different mix of cultures, though the same name and history continue. Longview Community Church in Phoenix, Arizona, saw its community change drastically over the years from an Anglo population to a Hispanic population. Seeing the change within the community, the church board decided to hire a Spanish-speaking associate pastor, who eventually became the senior pastor. This transition was possible because it was done with great respect for the heritage and history of the church and because a spirit of hospitality and generosity permeated the older congregation.

- *Advantage:* This model addresses the challenges of a changing community situation, and becoming outward-focused can reverse a radical decline.
- *Disadvantage:* This is a difficult model to engage unless the church and visionary leaders share a clear sense of urgency.

15. Catalytic Missionary Planter. A gifted church planter starts a new church, grows it to a group of 120 or so, and then calls in a founding pastor. The leader then moves on to repeat the process in other locations.

- *Advantages:* This model allows experienced and effective leaders to do what they do best: establish new congregations from birth to first pastor, similar to the approach of the apostle Paul in Acts. Up to one church a year can be started this way.
- *Disadvantages:* This model requires a full-time leader, which usually means a significant financial commitment. The transition from planter to first pastor can be difficult, and it requires people knowing from the beginning that the planter is a temporary servant.

16. Apostolic Regional Missionary (ARM). A highly gifted leader heads up a multiplication movement among a group of churches and leaders in a particular region. That leader gathers other planters and trains new leaders, who in turn plant churches and are coached by the ARM throughout the cycles of multiplication.

- *Advantage:* This model provides the most rapid results, with several churches being planted in a year.
- *Disadvantage:* This model requires a readiness to invest financially in the rapid expansion of the kingdom—more than $100,000 a year—so the values and structures of the local church and classis need to support planting.

Selecting a Planting Model

I hope this list of possible models has set off an explosion of possibilities in your imagination. As you move ahead, consider the following key factors in selecting a planting model that will best suit your situation:

- **Which model will best help you reach the underserved people God has placed on your heart?** If your target community is similar to the parent congregation, you might look closely at the multisite or hive-off models. If the target is distinctly different, you may be better served with a parachute plant.
- **Which model best leverages the resources you bring to the effort?** If you have a relationship with a strong, successful planter you may be able to send him or her out as an apostolic planter or regional missionary. If you're in a partnership with a church that is in decline or otherwise struggling, perhaps you can support it in a repotting or a relaunch. If you have a strong financial base or large group of people who desire to move out and start a new congregation, these realities will open possibilities in selecting your model.
- **Which model fits the gifts and calling of the church planter?** The vision of the planter will likely impact the target group and the planting model. If the planter is passionate about being bi-vocational and planting an organic church, deeply rooted in the planter's existing marketplace relationships, you might consider supporting a simple church network plant. Remember that a person with church

planting gifts will probably want to put his or her fingerprints on determining the target and method of planting.

- ❷ **Where does God seem to be moving?** It is always wise to gather people who are committed to advancing the mission of God's kingdom and seek their sense of where God is bringing together opportunity and resources. Their insights will likely give direction leading you to a model, a leader, and a target. Gain the wisdom of pastors, lay leaders, denominational leaders, and veteran planters.

Sometimes selecting a model for parenting comes into focus easily and the doors swing open. At other times the situation is less clear and takes time to discern. Invite as many people as possible into this process. Spend time in prayer and reflection. Give time for the above selection factors to "marinate." You will be amazed to discover how situations, options, and intentions come together in a wise model choice.

Next Step Questions

1. Which method of parenting planting seems best suited to serving the target group you sense God is leading you to reach?

2. Which method seems best suited to leveraging the resources you bring to the table?

3. Which method seems best suited to harmonizing with the gifts, vision, and talents of your planter and team?

4. Which method seems most in keeping with where God is moving?

5. Have you prayed about this to the extent that you feel you are truly open to where God is moving?

Chapter 8

Calling Your Lead Planter

"Leadership is translating vision into reality." —*Warren Bennis*

Two hours into an intense planter candidate evaluation, I began to get a sinking feeling. I could see that things were not going in a positive direction, and I knew it would be a big disappointment to many people if this candidate wasn't a good fit.

The candidate, who had flown in from across the country, had seemed to have all the right credentials. I had spoken with the pastor of the parent church weeks before, and he was already quite certain they had found their leader. Some remarkable things had happened, things that seemed like providential icing on the recruitment cake. As the date for our assessment interview approached, the enthusiasm for the planter only grew. A considerable investment on both sides, an impressive résumé, and the enthusiasm of respected leaders had created pressure for a positive endorsement.

The time had come for the behavioral interview, which is akin to running a fine-toothed comb through the experiences of the planter. Behavioral interviewing is vital in planter selection because the strongest predictor of future behavior is past behavior, and we have a fairly clear knowledge of which behaviors cause church planters to succeed. Listening to the candidate's responses to carefully formed questions, my heart sank further by the minute. We circled back and asked the questions again, hoping to hear the answers we wanted. The interview limped along for another few hours, after which we summarized our observations and parted company. I went to my office, closed the door, and wrote a draft summary report.

It is never easy to deliver a negative message when hopes are running high. As I sat with that parent church's pastor to go over my report, I was relieved to hear his agreement. He said, "Thanks—we had a sense that something might not be right." Relief! Thankfully this parent church had been through the emotional cycle of hiring before, so it had held back its heart commitment until receiving independent confirmation of the candidate. Far better to suffer a short-term hiring setback today than a long-term struggle on account of poor selection tomorrow! Even the planter agreed, sending a note a week later thanking us for the attention to detail and concurring with the outcome.

Most of us understand the importance of a hiring interview in leadership selection. What we may not appreciate is the importance of seeking objectivity in that assessment experience. Succumbing to the bias of individual intuition may put your whole plant project at great risk. Always get a third party to conduct the behavioral interview and produce a report with conclusions, and engage the decision process fully. Most church planting support agencies can help you find qualified, objective assessors.

All church planters, like all pastors, need a clear call from God to their ministry. This call is first heard internally, as an individual feels pulled toward church planting. But as all pastors and church leaders know, true calling is not just about internal, individual feelings and desires. A person's internal calling needs to be confirmed and affirmed by the external calling of others. The church plays a critical role in helping both potential planters and potential parent churches hear God's will and direction regarding the selection of the right planter. For a church planter, this external calling is the critical point at which others come alongside to evaluate, mutually discern, and consider God's will and direction.

The selection of the lead planter is the most important decision in a new church start. It cannot be overstated that this decision holds the greatest potential either of progressing your multiplication move or of hampering it. All too often this selection is done at a subconscious level in a moment of intuition and with a snap judgment. While that would be considered poor practice in the business world, in the church it is both risky and poor theological practice.

Following is a framework to use for successful planter selection. Each of these steps is crucial to a successful outcome.

Build a Planter Profile

Based on your insights into the likely target community, your congregational identity, the likely core group profile, the likely parenting model, and a sense of where God is moving, you should be able to outline a desired planter profile. That profile can include generational, educational, and geographical history, as well as ministry passion factors. Take time to do this work before you consider any candidate!

It is important, if you have been drawn to a planter candidate prior to this step, that you wipe the slate clean and work hard to build up a planter profile that would best (in human terms) minister to the people you seek to reach and plant with. After that work has been done well, you can open your search and selection to any interested and qualified candidates.

When you consider candidates for your position, one of the first steps is to request a résumé, a testimony of faith, and a statement of personal calling in ministry. These three resources can often help you quickly screen applicants for church planting as you consider their experience or personal commitment to Christ. If the candidate does not have a clear vision for planting a new church, you should probably not move forward with him or her. Church planting should never be "one of several equal options" in the mind of your candidate. He or she should have a clear sense of call to the work.

Determine the Candidate's Accountability to Your Denominational Judicatory

If your goal is to parent a new congregation that is within your Christian tradition and faithful to your denomination's beliefs, you need to know whether the planter is in fellowship (or willing to enter into fellowship) with the denomination and its local judicatory. Some time ago I was approached by a very gifted individual who had a successful track record in church planting. He was ready to plant again, but a few preliminary questions quickly revealed that he would not pass the standards of the local judicatory body of the denomination. So, after several conversations seeking to work through issues of theology, we had to part company. On other occasions (thankfully more common) individuals have come to us from other Christian traditions and, after healthy conversations, have been able to embrace and be embraced by the denomination.

Church planters are often dynamic people, and we are often drawn toward them with deep appreciation for their vision and winsome character. So it's best to discern early on whether a candidate will pass muster with your denominational standards. This is especially important if your church plant is being supported and sponsored by the denomination. I know a case in which a wonderful and vibrant church plant has grown into what most would call a healthy, established church. Nevertheless, there is some pain and frustration in denominational circles about the church's intentional distance from and dissonance with the denomination. Such pain and ecclesiastical disharmony could have been avoided if due diligence had been followed in the search process.

This is not to say that the only church plants worth investing in are those that fall in line with your particular denominational standards. God's kingdom is broad and wide and crosses over and through many denominational traditions. The point here is that when you select a church planter you need to be clear about your expectations.

Confirm Basic Pastoral Skills and Readiness to Minister

Church planting is tough work, requiring a skill set that relatively few individuals possess. Successful church planters are rarely found in their offices. They are out involved in public schools as a coach or at a Toastmasters group or on the street meeting the business leaders or teaching a class at a golf pro shop (one of my planter friends actually has that gig!) or volunteering as a chaplain in the local hospital. It is essential that they use their time this way so they can build the rich network of relationships needed for their core work of making disciples. They need to throw a wide net to form many relationships and then work those connections strategically.

That said, church planters are so busy learning and executing the planting skill set that they generally have little time to master basic pastoral skills. Planters who try to learn how to preach and lead while they learn how to plant will likely fail at both. Church planters need to be able to perform in these areas with a reasonable level of confidence and effectiveness before they take on planting. In other words, a reasonably experienced pastor who hears the call to plant a church is probably a better choice than the inexperienced pastor who needs to learn everything on the job.

Some time ago I talked with an aspiring church planter who needed thirty hours per week to get a sermon right. While gifted in many ways, he needed some additional time to build his confidence and efficiency in ministry before he took on the new skill set of planting. I am confident that day will come for this person and that he will be a very good communicator and planter. But a few more years to "sharpen the blade" will yield a much greater harvest!

This blade sharpening sometimes can be achieved while a person is being prepared and mentored in an established church. Many successful church planters have first honed their general pastoral craft as seminarians, interns, part-time pastors, and/or staff members working in established churches. The training and mentoring they receive may not give them all the church planting tools they will need, but it gives them good insight into and experience in general pastoral work. It also provides an opportunity for a church contemplating church planting to see a potential planter in action. Both the planter and the planting church learn to know and understand one another.

Engage an Expert to Conduct a Behavioral Interview and Write a Report

Arranging for a solid and certified behavioral interview is an essential step in church planter selection. Behavioral interviewing is based on a simple premise: the strongest predictor of future behavior is past behavior. The core behaviors of successful church planters are fairly well known as a result of research done in this area that has proved valid across ethnic, gender, and generational boundaries. It is possible, therefore, to discern a gifted planter with some accuracy by "drilling down" into their lives in search of matching behavioral qualities.

The work of sifting through a candidate's life and work requires significant training to ensure a reliable report. Good assessors have been trained and mentored in candidate selection over many years. They pay close attention to both the carefully outlined behavioral norms and standards and the techniques of interviewing. They are not interested in a candidate's theories or thoughts of what he or she might do or could do if hired as a planter. They are only interested in past behavior and how that lays a pattern of predictable behavior in the future. Both your top candidate and, if married, his or her spouse should go through this process; your local church planting consultant can likely point you to an agency equipped to do the work for a reasonable fee. These are the best dollars you will spend by far!

Following is a brief outline of the thirteen categories that Charles Ridley developed for planter selection discernment. These dimensions have been tested in university-based research and are the standard for most planter selection work today.

Primary Categories:

1. Visioning capacity: Generates vision, initiates plants, and builds significant projects from the ground floor up.
2. Intrinsic motivation: Demonstrates the ability to be a self-starter who works with diligence and excellence.
3. Creating ownership of ministry: Passes on the baton of ministry to others so they can continue the race.
4. Reaching the unchurched: Consistently reaches out to the unchurched and influences them toward a relationship with Christ and his church.
5. Spousal support: Collaborates with spouse as a team in marriage and ministry.

The first five categories are often called the "knock-out categories," as they are core critical patterns in a planter's life. If a candidate lacks strong evidence of any one of these five qualities, it is doubtful he or she should be assessed positively as having church planting gifts and promise.

Secondary Categories:

6. Effectively builds relationships: Evidences the ability to meet new people and engage them in relationships at varied depths.
7. Committed to church growth: Embraces growing the church, both numerically and spiritually, and implements church growth principles in an effective manner.
8. Responsive to community: Understands local communities and implements culturally responsive ministries.
9. Utilizes the giftedness of others: Assesses, develops, and releases others to serve in their areas of giftedness.
10. Flexible: Negotiates change successfully, while staying centered on the overall vision.
11. Builds cohesive groups: Helps widely differing people function as a unified body.
12. Resilient: Stays the course in the face of major setbacks, disappointments, and opposition.
13. Exercises faith: Evidences a strong and vital relationship with God and demonstrates a willingness to take significant faith risks.

After the behavioral interview, the assessor or assessors should write up a detailed report. That report should have the approval of all parties—assessor(s) and candidate—and you should treat it as a confidential document, not to be released apart from the conclusions. Treating the candidate's full disclosure with respect is an essential factor in building a foundation of trust between you.

The assessor's report should make a recommendation, though in some cases a "conditionally recommended" response will be indicated, in which case you should be sure the planter is able to meet the conditions outlined.

To emphasize how critical this interview is, a study by Stephen Gray candidates who were "marginal" in their final assessment were far more likely to plant a struggling church than those who were strongly recommended (*Planting Fast-growing Churches*, Church Smart, 2007, pp. 59-60). This insight should give pause to a casual attitude toward an interview report.

The church seeking a church planter does not need to fully understand all the categories and judgments involved in a behavioral interview. That's what the experts are for. In many cases your denomination will be more than willing and able to walk you through the process, make referrals, and, in some cases, even pay for the evaluation and report. Don't be afraid to lean heavily on those who can come alongside you with needed support.

Check References

Reference checking is standard hiring practice for most industries, although it is remarkable to me how often this step gets put off until the very end and then is glossed over. References confirm that the candidate has the good character and skills to lead a new ministry. Focusing on character and competence will give you significant insight into the individual you are considering.

Each candidate should provide three to five references. When you contact the references, ask open-ended questions to give them plenty of room to share their experience with the individual. If the individual is unknown to you or comes from outside your denomination, it is especially important to do careful reference checking. Some years back a potential planter moved through many stages of the assessment process with flying colors. We nearly missed the significant character issue that ultimately disqualified him from planting with our team. He went ahead and planted a church on his own, and in a few short months the community discerned and reacted against his character flaws.

Discern the Planter's Environmental Risk

Dr. Tom Nebel is the director of church planting for Converge, which describes itself as "a movement of churches working together to strengthen and start more churches." Tom has worked hard for many years to lower the risk in church planting, and in so doing he has identified objective assessment and coaching as two key steps in that direction. He has also identified what he calls "environmental risk." A full description of this can be found in *Parent Church Landmines* (Ben Ingebretson and Tom Nebel, Church Smart, 2009). That publication also has a helpful assessment exercise and scale to facilitate more accurate discernment.

Environmental risk is determined by four strong factors and four moderate factors. The strong factors are as follows:

1. How will the plant be funded? Full funding lowers the risk, while bi-vocation or "living by faith" raises the risk.
2. How closely does the site approximate the background of the planter? Strong similarity lowers the risk, while great dissimilarity raises it.
3. How many ministry partners will move with the planter? Having none raises the risk, while five or more significantly reduces the risk.
4. How many preexisting adult contacts are in the area? None raises the risk, while five or more significantly reduces the risk.

Moderate risk factors are as follows:

1. How near does your family live to the site? Nearby reduces the risk, while significant distance raises the risk.
2. How close is the site to your geographical roots? Nearby reduces the risk, while great distance raises the risk.
3. How close are you to churches that support your work? Nearby reduces the risk, while distance raises it.
4. How much vocational success have you experienced in ministry? Much reduces the risk, while little or none raises it.

Environmental risk analysis helps discern whether a planter can take on a particular challenge. Remember that several factors can be adjusted to lower the risk. For example, if the planter is being considered before a final site and demographic for the plant have been determined, you can lower the environmental risk by choosing a site for the plant that is near the planter's family and near the churches that support the work. On the other hand, if the site and demographics have already been firmly established, you can lower the environmental risk by looking for a church planter who has geographical roots in that area. The point is to make sure you are aware of what the risks are and whether or not you are willing to live with them.

Determine the Planter's Financial and Marital Health

Last night I sat with a search team that interviewed a planter candidate with great promise. In the course of the interview we asked about his ability to relocate into the target community. With eyes lowered, the candidate shared that his family was "upside down" in their mortgage and would not be able to make a move for several years as they tried to catch up financially.

These are difficult financial times, both for the countries of the world and for individuals. While the advance of the gospel cannot be dictated by these circumstances, it is wise to make them a part of the overall selection process. Church planters rarely do good work if they are stressed by financial trouble. Whether that financial stress is the result of cumulative misfortune or poor choices it can create such a distraction that the planter cannot perform at maximum effectiveness. While this is sensitive ground and needs to be strictly confidential, it is important to interview both planter and spouse as to their financial health.

When a couple's income-to-debt ratio exceeds 35 percent, there is a significant likelihood that it will create stress in their relationship. Of course, no two situations are alike, and the collapse of the real estate market has created uniquely difficult circumstances. Getting a handle on debt and developing the stewardship integrity that comes from that can take years, but the result is a capacity to lead that is essential in most planting environments.

Marital health, if applicable, is another area that needs close attention in planter selection; since this issue is similarly sensitive, exercise confidentiality here as well. Church planters do not have the luxury of a compartmentalized life in which they have routinely defined working hours and separate business phone lines that don't ring on evenings and weekends. The support of the planter's spouse is essential to the planter's success.

Charles Ridley and Tweed Moore have identified five key qualities of a strong planter marriage:

1. The couple has a clear understanding of, and commitment to, their roles in ministry and what they expect from each other.

2. They have established firm boundaries regarding all aspects of church and family life.
3. This couple evidences a solid, godly, bomb-proof marriage. Their love and commitment to one another shine through clearly.
4. Their communication is open, honest, and timely. They listen well to one another and actively put the other's needs before their own.
5. Both husband and wife are united in their desire for church planting. They are actively supporting one another in preparing for the possibility of church planting.

—Evaluating and Reporting, Church Smart Resources, 2000, p. 134.

Both the financial and the marital strength of the couple should be evaluated by a trained assessment team. If you are the hiring agency, you should have a full and detailed report on how the couple scored and how the assessors judge their fitness to plant in light of these critical areas.

In addition to criteria like the five key qualities listed above, there are several other behaviorally-based selection tools available. They all accept the premise that past behaviors hold the key to planter selection. Still, no matter how good your assessment tools are, good old-fashioned personal relationships and the experiences of those who know the individual planter and spouse are as valuable a tool as any other. If you do not know a perspective planter personally, you need to talk to those who do. And if you do know the planter and his or her spouse personally, ask yourself what you have observed and felt. If there are any areas of concern, call them out openly with the prospective planter. Don't make the mistake of thinking that past behaviors will be transformed because of a new position and venue.

Other Gift, Personality, and Psychological Assessments

There are many other instruments and assessment tools that you can use in working with candidates for ministry. Spiritual gift inventories are helpful in gaining a picture of the individual. Spiritual gifts of leadership and evangelism are often high on the list of those who aspire to plant. Evidence of those gifts will come out in the behavioral interview, which also weights them heavily. A person who truly has those gifts will also demonstrate the fruit of them in his or her life, and that is the acid test!

An assessment called the APEST seeks to discern which of the Ephesians 4:11 equipping gifts the planter manifests. Those gifts are "apostolic, prophetic, evangelistic, shepherding, and teaching." Often, but not always, church planters will assess high in the area of apostolic leadership and evangelism. Again, the behavioral interview will reveal these if they are truly present in the candidate. Personality assessments should be weighted more lightly. The fact is that there is a marvelous diversity of personalities among church planters. Some are gregarious extroverts; others, not so much so. Personality assessments are not a primary tool for planter assessment.

Psychological inventories are important for all clergy at some point in their training. This is usually part of the seminary experience. If you are working with a pastor who has been to seminary, it is likely that he or she has had this work done and you will not need to repeat it. With more planters coming into this work from nontraditional paths, however, it can be wise to invest in this element of the process. The MMPI (Minnesota Multiphasic Psychological Inventory) or a similar tool can quickly red-flag concerns in the areas of depression, hyper control, inability to trust, or problems in forming strong relationships.

Confirm Vision Alignment of Planter and Parent

Most important, seek to discern the vision for planting that lies in the heart and mind of your candidate and how strongly he or she holds that vision. Many will have some vision of the kind of plant to which they are drawn. Some hold deep convictions about this, while others will be more open and eager to discover the vision of the parent congregation. Asking the question early can go a long way toward reducing tension and creating clarity down the road.

Some time back I watched a carefully-designed parenting plan collide with a planter's vision that was not fully disclosed during the early phase of the relationship. Both parties were frustrated with one another as time progressed. One solution to this problem is to be flexible as a parent congregation and not develop the plan in detail until the planter is on board. The better solution lies with understanding each other's vision through careful interviewing and conversation.

There is no substitute for simply spending time together. This is the customary, time-honored way search teams, pastors, and congregational members best discern whether or not God is leading them to call or accept a call to serve in a specific location.

A Few Thoughts on Planting Teams

A quick read of the book of Acts confirms the presence of "apostolic teams" as a success pattern in the early church. Church planting teams can be tremendous sources of high motivation, mutual support, daily accountability, and mental stimulation. I have seen them work wonderfully, particularly when the players have had several years of close friendship prior to the teaming and there are clearly defined roles and responsibilities.

In most cases the overall cost of the planting plan will go up when you deploy a team, though there are exceptions. I watched a team of two in my area do tremendous work in their new church start, each taking half of the salary. Andy and Chris had been friends for years prior to their planting project, and they had an honest and fair appraisal of their relative strengths. Because they both placed a high value on being deeply connected to their community through other vocational work, it was easy to split one salary. Other teams seek to raise full salaries for both planters in anticipation of a large launch.

There are, however, pitfalls to teaming that are worth noting. One is the little problem of ego. Working in a team setting demands maturity and humility. If the partners have developed a working friendship prior to the planting partnership, they are likely to have a more stable and healthy relationship. Be careful, however, of those who have had a nonworking friendship. A friendship that may be genuine but has never been tested by a close working relationship tells you very little about the likelihood of success. I know a couple of school buddies who studied together, hung out together, and dreamed of planting a church together. But once they were in the church planting environment, they found they didn't work together well. Whether in the church or business world, partnerships present challenges that demand careful, thoughtful, and prayerful discernment.

Another factor arises when one (or both) teammates does not have all the core qualities needed to pass an assessment interview. In these cases a planting team, or parent congregation lead team, may argue that the deficiencies of one team member are compensated for by the other. This is undoubtedly true to some degree. However, both team members should always have all of the primary behavioral competencies. The visibility of their role, along with the need to embody these key qualities, requires it.

Church planter assessment is time-consuming and detailed work. It involves significant cost, but it is worth every dime. No other decision you make will be as significant as planter selection.

Next Steps: Planter Selection Checklist

☐ Build planter profile

☐ Receive résumé, testimony, and vision for ministry/calling

☐ Determine whether planter is accountable to denominational authority

☐ Confirm presence of basic pastoral skills

☐ Perform objective behavioral interview

☐ Complete reference check

☐ Discern environmental risk

☐ Determine financial and marital health

☐ Discern right fit to your planting context

☐ Perform other gift, personality, and psychological assessments

☐ Discern vision alignment of parent and planter

Chapter 9

Release, Support, and Recovery

"Don't cry because it is over; smile because it happened!" —Dr. Seuss

It has been a bit of a tough year at my house. For the last twenty-five years I have been up to my elbows in parenting three kids into adulthood. It has been a great experience, with lots of fun and chaos along the way. We made great memories and cemented our love for one another deeply through the significant events as well as the humdrum routines of life.

But now the kids are gone and things have definitely changed. They grew up and moved out into the world without me. It has been exciting to see each of the kids mature and choose a path beyond high school out into adulthood. Granted, it's a bit bumpy at first. They come home on weekends, are carried on my insurance, call to talk about car troubles, and arrive home for the holidays with that big white laundry bag! But I love to see them come home; the house seems empty without them.

Most parents recognize that the season of "empty nesting" requires that they explore new avenues of development for themselves (there *is* a life after 24/7 parenting!). Releasing your children is emotional work. It requires a new style of relating as you shift from the intense season of direct parenting to the new opportunities life brings in a new season.

Parenting a new congregation is remarkably similar to parenting a child during the transition into adulthood and beyond. There is emotional, relational, and developmental work to be done. In this chapter we take a look at the elements of transition (release, support, and recovery) that will help you move forward as a healthy parent and a new church plant.

Wise Release

Just as parents need to learn to let their children go, parent churches need to let the churches they plant grow and thrive on their own.

I once heard a pastor describe the difficult experience of letting go. His congregation had planted several new churches, but each time they did so this pastor felt a strong dislike for the name the plant chose for itself. Each time he was tempted to jump in and control that decision, but he checked his reaction. Sure enough, eventually he came to accept and like the names of the new churches that had sprouted, and he successfully avoided the trap of being overbearing.

Failure to fully release a new start from its parent congregation can create resentment or dependency, and neither is good! Here are three important things to know about releasing your new church plant.

1. Releasing your planter means allowing him or her to give full energy to the task of leading the new plant. When your planter returns from boot camp (the intensive one- or two-week planting preparation experience most planters undergo), he or she will begin refining the strategy for developing the plant. As that happens, it becomes increasingly important to shift your role. The sooner you begin to release decision-making authority to the planter and the teams the planter develops, the better!

It can be tempting to get the church planter overly involved with tasks that are important to the parent church, particularly if you are using a model in which the church planter is hired as a staff member of the parent church. But the planter needs time and freedom to do the prelaunch work and to recruit a core group, if that is in keeping with your plant model. To do this work effectively, the planter must be released from all other responsibilities.

Giving the planter freedom to build relationships with both leaders and givers from within the parent church is critical at this stage. Creating intercessory prayer teams to surround the planter and the plan, giving the planter visibility with regular preaching opportunities, and planning social gatherings are all integral to that process.

2. Release means letting go of valued members of your congregation. Again, assuming that developing a core group is congruent with your parenting model, the parent church must be willing to joyfully release those who will join the new church plant. This is very hard for the staff and congregation of the parent church to do. One church used the phrase "We must give away our very best to God's kingdom" as we talked about who would leave the parent church to go to the new church plant. They insisted on giving away their "firstfruits."

One word of warning here. Do not make the fatal mistake of announcing, "Anyone is welcome to join the launch team or core group of our new church plant." It's far better to work with your planter to develop a selection and interview process whereby the planter can recruit key people for the ministry teams from those who are spiritually and otherwise mature. Too often a core group is frustrated and derailed by one individual who is overly "needy" or unable to be a positive contributor to the plant. Your new church start will have difficulty getting on its feet and growing if it is forced to direct its attention away from the people it is seeking to reach and serve. Spending time with the planter to "prequalify" individuals the planter can recruit for the core group is a wise strategy that will increase the likeliness of a strong start. Take extra time for this, as it is a key way to set up the planting leader for success. Of course, people will make choices and the new ministry will likely include some individuals who need extra care. The important thing is to be sure there is adequate strength to create healthy momentum.

From Jim

At New Hope it was hard on our worship director and the entire congregation when almost half of our worship team left for our new church plant. That was a significant loss for a church of only 200. However, God quickly provided others from within the congregation who had wanted to be part of the worship team but thought they would never get the chance.

3. Release must happen at the appropriate time. If you release your plant before the funding plan is clear, reasonable, and agreed upon, your release is too soon. If you release your plant before the planter has been prepared through boot camp and an established coach relationship (this is really critical!), your release is too soon. If you release your plant before there are at least 40 committed, spiritually healthy and mature people in the core group and you intend for the plant to be self-sustaining inside of four years, your release is too soon. Releasing too late, on the other hand, can also have a limiting impact on the plant, as people will wander off the team or otherwise become disillusioned with the vision if it is unnecessarily drawn out. Timing matters!

Wise Support

Supporting your new church plant certainly involves the gifts of prayer, finances, and personnel. It can also involve providing office furniture and computer equipment or stocking a nursery with toys and changing tables. In Appendix D we've provided a comprehensive listing of resources a new plant may need. At a deeper level, however, a church plant needs helpful structures, advocacy, counsel, and wisdom in order to thrive. A governing team, a planter coach, and a parent/planter covenant are perhaps the three best ongoing support systems you can offer to help establish a new congregation.

The Governing Team

My observation is that a significant portion of church planters are not gifted in organizational development. Planters tend to get their energy from people and relationships. They work hard at networking and then seek to develop programming to capture those relationships in spiritual formation and discipleship. The result is that the church plant's oversight and governance structures are neglected. When we refer to "oversight and governance," we are addressing what an organized congregation would call their council, consistory, or board.

Neglecting to develop a governing team can seem minor in the early phases of planting, when people are swept up in the excitement of launching the ministry. When the ministry faces a challenge, however, that neglect can be fatal. If you are using the multisite model, then the oversight is likely carried out within the parent church's board or consistory. If not, it is imperative that your plant form its own governing board. It is always best when the planter takes the lead in forming the governing team and initiating monthly meetings with an appropriate agenda. If the planter does not do so, it may be necessary for the parent church to spark the formation of the team.

Following is a summary of the role and makeup of the governing team and an excellent agenda format for monthly meetings:

- ❷ Ensure that the original intent, design, and timeframes of the plant are maintained, unless otherwise agreed.
- ❷ Ensure the fiscal integrity and health of the plant by reviewing the budget and income and supporting necessary external fundraising.

- Address any major personnel issues, including an annual review of the planter.
- Provide avenues for major stakeholders to express concerns and receive updates.
- See to the spiritual welfare of the planter and the planted congregation.

It is important to understand that the role of the team is to hold the planter accountable without micromanaging. Accountability means providing oversight and governance that is founded on trust, clear boundaries, and agreed-upon expectations. Practicing this approach begins the minute you confirm the lead planter hire. The parent may make suggestions and provide input, but it should be communicated as such.

Trust is a critical quality to nurture between parent and plant. Extending trust to the planter means that he or she has the freedom to develop the plant within the following boundaries:

- theological and biblical integrity
- professional ministry ethics
- budgetary capabilities
- expectations of progress benchmarks
- accountability to an oversight team, coach, and ecclesial body

Inside these boundaries the planter is free to creatively lead while remaining responsible to demonstrate the outcomes to which both parties have agreed. Stephen Gray has these strong words on this subject:

> Church planters in the field have a clear understanding of the needs of the community and how the new church can address those needs. They are the eyes and ears on the street. They hear the daily gripes and joys of their budding congregation. They are living it. An individual in a headquarters building [or in the planting church] is not as intimately connected to the community being served. Once the location is chosen and some initial demographics are completed, I believe the church planter should have full control.
>
> —*Planting Fast-growing Churches*, Church Smart, 2005, p. 78.

This principle is not an easy one for those in established churches and leadership structures to understand. Established churches often have layers of tradition, policies, and procedures within which everyone and everything must function. Moreover, pastors in these churches are usually proud of these practices and have found them to be successful.

From Paul

It can be hard to see a "child" intentionally make different choices than the parents would make. But in my own setting at Brookside Christian Reformed Church, we give as much latitude and freedom as possible, trusting the church planter and encouraging him to "find his own way." In short, it is my conviction that parent churches need to cast the boundaries widely enough that the church planter and the new congregation can spread their wings and fly. Once again, this is not all that different from what good, thoughtful parents do for their children. As the old adage goes, "Give your children both roots and wings."

This emphasis on extending trust and freedom to the planter has a balancing factor: accountability. Accountability can be expressed both in terms of deadlines (when the parent would like to see the plant offering public worship or concluding outside funding, for example) and in terms of numerical benchmarks. Those benchmarks can be reported on monthly or quarterly and can relate to contacts with unchurched people, leadership development, fundraising, oversight team meetings, and worship attendance. Benchmarks can be both process- and result-oriented. They should be outlined prior to confirming a plant hire but then refined as you release the new ministry. If the plant falls seriously behind in reaching agreed-upon benchmarks, it may become necessary for the governing team (in which the parent has a part) to assert more control.

The governance team should include the following persons:

- ❷ the planter, who serves as chairperson
- ❷ a representative of the parent church, usually the pastor
- ❷ a denominational/local representative
- ❷ an experienced church planting adviser
- ❷ a finance person (at times this role can be provided by the parent until the plant can provide it)
- ❷ a mature layperson from the church plant core team.

Some of these roles can be doubled up; for example, the denominational leader may also be an experienced planting adviser, or the layperson from the plant can be the finance person. Over time (say two to four years) the members of the governance team often will be replaced by indigenous leaders from the plant.

Coaching

Having a coach or mentor available for the church planter can dramatically impact the success of a new plant. The coach is a confidential asset to the planter, helping him or her think through often-complex priorities. A wise and sensitive coach brings out the best in a planter and can guide him or her through challenges while staying focused on the main objectives. Coaching for church planters is best if it is a blend of content-neutral accountability and ministry processing, along with content-rich best practice wisdom. My friend Tom Nebel believes coaching can raise the survival and success rate of a church plant by 20 percent!

Unfortunately, coaching often gets overlooked in the overall ministry plan for a new church. This can be true because the planter is seeking to make the best use of every dollar at his or her disposal, and coaching does not seem to rise to the level of "critical." A key support role a parent can play, one that will pay dividends many times over, is to fund the coaching role for the first three to four years. With an annual cost of $1,000 to $2,000, funding a coach is a relatively modest expense with lasting impact.

It is important to find a coach who can truly be a neutral "safe person." While some senior pastors are equipped to serve as coaches, this arrangement is not usually helpful. Navigating the dynamics between the senior pastor and the planter can be tricky, and a third party is often needed to help. For example, if the planter is not getting enough "face time" in front of the congregation to properly communicate the planting vision, the planter may need coaching from a third party on how to talk to the senior pastor.

Planter/Parent Covenant

Another key element in releasing the church plant is drafting a planter/ parent covenant. When both parties have clear and written expectations they are more likely to have a successful relationship. Following are the key components of a good covenant:

1. Commitments of the parent to the planter, including:
   a. prayer and advocacy.
   b. financial and resource commitments.
   c. open communication and trust building.
2. Commitments of the planter to the parent, including:
   a. accountability to agreed-upon benchmarks through monthly oversight meetings.
   b. honoring the sacrifice of resources through careful management.
   c. open communication and trust building.
3. Shared commitments to decision making relative to
   a. the objective, target, and general timelines of the plant.
   b. the financial design of the plant.
   c. the staffing evaluation.

—Ben Ingebretson and Tom Nebel, *Parent Church Landmines*,
Church Smart, 2009, pp. 97-98.

Don't hesitate to spend considerable time in framing this covenant, since it will serve as a guide for the expectations of everyone involved. Should it become clear over time that some of the stipulations in the covenant are unnecessary or don't work well, both parties can always agree to revise the covenant.

Wise Recovery

Parenting a new church stretches everyone involved. What is often a surprise is the fact that when the stretching is over the parent congregation rarely returns to the same ministry dimension it had before. If the parent was committed to the multiplication values going into birthing, whatever losses it experienced in terms of gifted members or finances quickly rebound. If evangelism, leadership development, and other multiplication values were weak, it may take longer. But most congregations are surprised by how a multiplication move increases the energy and growth of the parent. At the very least, after parenting they see ministry in new ways. Generativity, that quality that focuses on empowerment and leadership development, will likely have become more central to their vision and heart. Passion for evangelism and outreach will be on the rise as the new congregation feeds back its energy for evangelism into the parent congregation through stories and testimonies. Parenting is a stretch, but the outcome is a renewed vision for ministry in the parent church!

Even given all the potential positive outcomes in parenting, every multiplication move requires a recovery phase. That recovery has several dimensions, as outlined by Bob Logan and Steve Ogne.

1. The first step in recovery is rest. Recognize those who have worked overtime in the birthing process and give them rest. Give the church time to recover. When the celebration ends and the recovery is well underway, be ready with a new vision for future ministry.

2. Emotional recovery—Giving birth requires a lot of physical and emotional energy. Plan for a period of rest and renewal following the birth. The grand opening of the new church is like the birth of a child and the marriage of that child at the same time. When it comes to churches, you often give them away on the same day they are born.

3. Attendance growth—It will usually take three months to a year to [recover attendance at the parent church] if 10% of your average attendance is given to the new church. This assumes that the parent church is involved in effective outreach and assimilation. Lack of recovery is an indicator of weak evangelism and assimilation systems.

4. Financial recovery—The time required for financial recovery will vary depending on the number of tithers [who have moved from the parent to the plant] and the length of time you committed to funding the project. Remember, it is impossible to out-give God. . . . Watch for his creative blessings.

5. Leadership development—It will usually take three months to a year to raise up new leaders and workers to replace those given to the new congregation. This is a positive process that results in more people being mobilized in ministry. Apprenticing of replacement leaders should begin during the conception and prenatal phases. Lack of new leaders indicates the lack of a system to challenge, train, and mobilize people for ministry.

—*Churches Planting Churches*, Church Smart, 1995, p. 12-6.

One helpful strategy at this stage of the parenting cycle is to use a church health assessment tool to help you survey the wider ministry and focus your recovery energy. Natural Church Development can be a very effective means to accomplish that. You can find more information on NCD online at ncd-international.org.

Finally, this is a time to look over your entire ministry with fresh multiplication eyes. How might every dimension of the ministry experience a multiplying dynamic? Can every leader mentor another? Can you deepen multiplication values during this recovery season, when people are paying close attention to the parenting of a new church?

Successes and Setbacks

As the parenting church goes through the recovery process, it's important to celebrate successes and empathize with the setbacks of the church plant. A parent church's support is a great boost to morale, whether celebrating the first service of the plant or struggling with the loss of a key family.

Every positively assessed church planter is exceptional as a person and pastor, but he or she is asked to take on tremendous challenges and risks. Developing momentum in a new church start can at times feel like moving a ton of bricks uphill, and what may seem like modest and meager progress can come at a great price. Celebrate often and support your planter with words and gestures of encouragement!

Church planters often face challenges and setbacks that test their resolve. Sometimes the setbacks are the result of poor choices (like the planter who tried to plant an urban Goth-themed church in a rural community), sometimes they're the result of misfortune (like the planter who could only find worship space on Saturday night), and sometimes setbacks come because of sinful behavior (a planter falls into a gambling addiction and begins to embezzle funds). Planters do their work in the same fallen world we all share.

The book of Acts gives us a helpful "theology of setback" as a reminder of the predictable challenges that will come, as well as an encouragement for how the story ultimately ends. Acts begins with a great season of growth on the day of Pentecost, as thousands convert to Christ (Acts 2:14ff). Shortly after that, however, there is a setback in the form of persecution (Acts 4:1-22), but that setback leads to growth and development of the Christian community (Acts 4:23ff). There is another setback in the sin of Ananias and Sapphira (Acts 5:1-11), but that situation again leads to spiritual power and ministry after the sin is addressed (Acts 5:12ff). Once again the community is faced with a setback of religious opposition (Acts 5:17-18), and once again the setback becomes a platform for a surge forward in gospel ministry through preaching and new partnerships (Acts 5:19ff).

The cycle of advance, setback, and advance repeats itself throughout the book of Acts. Each time a setback becomes a foundation for a new surge forward. This "theology of setback" is the Christian way: death comes before resurrection. As a parent church, support your planter with an awareness of these cycles of celebration and setback, particularly in the early days when the setbacks can sting powerfully.

Finally, during the recovery phase, be sure to chronicle what you have experienced and learned through the process. Having birthed a new church, you are now far more likely to birth again! What you do today to capture the lessons and insights from the lead team can help you have an even more effective and positive experience next time.

Final Steps Questions

1. What dimension of releasing (planter, people, or resources) will be most difficult for you, and what will you need to do to complete this task?

2. How can you support your new church plant without smothering it or otherwise exercising unhealthy control?

3. What recovery work do you need to do? Where do you need to focus your energy?

4. How will you celebrate successes and mourn setbacks with the church plant?

5. How has this experience challenged you to build multiplication values and practice into every ministry area of your church?

6. What have you learned through the parenting experience? What debriefing process do you need to engage in to set a healthy course toward the future and toward your next multiplication move?

Chapter 10

Conclusion: A Tale of Two Church Plants

"It was the best of times; it was the worst of times." —Charles Dickens

In 2003 I made my first visit to Lewis Center, Ohio, a suburb of Columbus. Lewis Center was projected to be a high-growth area by every demographic study, and as I drove the area I could see the outlines of new subdivisions and strip malls. The church planters who had accepted the challenge to work there had come more than 200 miles east to do the job. Dave and Vicki Jansen were seasoned in ministry and had a clear call to plant a new church in the north Ohio community. The Jansens were "parachute planters." There was no proximal parent church to Lewis Center, so this was pioneer work. Dave and Vicki moved into the community with little more than the training they had received and their family of four. With no cluster of partners awaiting their arrival, those were some solitary months.

The early years of the Jansens' work in Lewis Center were not easy, but Dave and Vicki did everything right for planters who were starting from scratch: they networked with community leaders, met with other pastors, befriended their neighbors. Knowing that the clock was ticking on their funding, they worked hard to advertise in Lewis Center with flyers, radio spots, and mailings. Little by little, bit by bit, they inched forward, adding a few people each year.

Unfortunately those were also years of loss, as some people became discouraged when they saw how slow it can be to plant a church from scratch. At one point, Dave began to wonder if the fledgling effort would survive. One Sunday there were more people up front in the worship team than in the congregation! Despite the struggle, faithfulness and hard work—infused with God's grace—yielded a harvest. Dave and Vicki saw their dream unfold, with an organized congregation named Center Point and a daycare center in their own building. Today they are thriving in ministry, but they haven't forgotten the difficult years.

Fast forward to 2010. I received a call from Dave one day, and there was energy in his voice. I knew Dave was made of church planter stuff, but when I put the phone down that day I discovered that Dave was also an apostolic leader. He told me about Jonathan, a small-business owner whom Dave had been discipling. Jonathan had felt a call to ministry and wanted to plant a new church himself. As I listened to the story Dave poured out over the phone, I clearly heard that Jonathan's vision was exactly what Dave had been hoping for. Dave did not want to plant one church. He did not even want to plant one mega-church. Dave wanted to spark a multiplication of churches in the Columbus area, and Jonathan's interest provided hope of the second-generation church plant that Dave had envisioned from the start.

I recently spent time with Dave and Jonathan to get an update on how the new plant was unfolding in Westerville, Ohio. Jonathan was well along in his theological training, and the new plant had already begun public worship after a few months of pre-launch. Dave shared how Center Point had sent many of its best people to make up the core group of the Westerville campus. As a result, a few months into public worship the new church was light-years ahead of where the mother church had been at the same time in its early months. Where Dave had started with nothing, Jonathan was blessed with momentum as the result of having a parent congregation. As I listened to Jonathan tell the stories of new faces and the energy of Sundays, Dave smiled and said, "A parent church makes a huge difference!"

Parenting Is the Difference

Church planting is a key element of God's mission to meet the spiritual hunger in North America today. In almost every case, new churches with invested parent congregations are more likely to thrive than those that don't have a parent. They do so because of the momentum that comes from the powerful effect of partnering with people who are able to share the tasks and joys of ministry. Parenting churches make all the difference for planters like Dave and Jonathan who have a vision for church multiplication.

What would be the impact if every church in North America invested in parenting other congregations? Inactive and under-challenged laypeople would step up in new ways. Inwardly focused churches would become energized afresh for community ministry. Churches that have not seen an adult baptism in years would begin to long for and experience this. A much higher percentage of church plants would thrive and multiply themselves that much sooner. Stronger church plants would better be able to reach new people with the message of Christ.

Recently I had occasion to spend time with George Bullard, a widely published and well-known denominational consultant. George told me about a time when he was seeking to plant hundreds of new churches. In that effort George linked every church that was hoping to parent with two other congregations. Those additional churches were given the opportunity to support the new church plant in multiple ways and to learn the parenting process without the full obligation to parent themselves. They were in training and later would become parents themselves with two understudies of their own.

What would be the impact if every parent church mentored two other congregations, who then learned the parenting moves so that they "caught the bug" and developed the confidence to parent themselves? New parent congregations would spring up as never before in North America. Congregations would catch an enthusiasm for multiplication that cannot be generated in any other way. Leaders would discover as never before their God-given design for "generativity" and fruitfulness. Pastors would discover a new bond in ministry as they leverage their resources for the next generation.

God has called us all to bring his blessing into the world through planting new churches. Bearing "much fruit . . . fruit that remains" is our call (John 15:8, 16). May we know the special joy that comes in helping bring in the kingdom harvest. May our parenting efforts make a difference in the lives of other pastors and church planters, and, above all, in the lives of people to whom God wants to spread the blessing of his covenant.

Action Steps for a Parenting Church

First Phase: Prepare

Step 1: Map your starting point (Chapter 1)

- Gauge the congregation's commitment level.
- Build trust as a foundation to action.
- Seek God's will with an eye toward where God is already moving.

Step 2: Make the Case to Parent (Chapter 2)

- Discover the biblical, demographic, strategic, and pragmatic reasons to parent.
- Develop a case and prepare a winsome presentation.

Second Phase: Engage

Step 1: Build a Lead Team and Engage the Congregation (Chapter 3)

- Define the purpose of the team
- Recruit a lead team of qualified people.
- Develop team trust.
- Orient the team to the parenting process.
- Engage the congregation in the vision for parenting.

Step 2: Navigate Hidden Forces (Chapter 4)

- Address the parenting congregation's fears.
- Identify the congregation's existing values and develop parenting values.
- Address resistance to change.

- Develop prayer energy and strategy.
- Use "force field analysis" to gain perspective.

Step 3: Develop a Sustainable Funding Plan (Chapter 5)

- Develop a preliminary funding plan that will bring the plant to sustainability in three to four years.
- Develop a preliminary budget and define revenue sources.
- Discern your approach to risk management.
- Set up the planter for funding success.

Third Phase: Establish

Step 1: Discern a Planting Opportunity (Chapter 6)

- Determine general need in your community.
- Discern your congregation's capacity for "cultural reach."
- Leverage tools to discern best potential target group.
- Make room for planter input and Spirit leading.

Step 2: Select a Parenting Model (Chapter 7)

- Consider a range of parenting options.
- Select a model based on integrating principles.
- Seek confirmation of parenting model through prayer.

Step 3: Call a Lead Planter (Chapter 8)

- Build a planter profile based on potential target group.
- Determine potential candidates' accountability to denominational judicatory, basic pastoral skills, environmental risk, financial and marital health.
- Check references.
- Arrange for an expert assessment of the chosen candidate and employ other assessment tools.
- Confirm vision alignment of planter and parenting church.

Fourth Phase: Release

Step 1: Release the Planting Team (Chapter 9)

- Release the planter for full-time planting work.
- Release members from the congregation to the plant through selection process.
- Release a wide range of resources to the plant.

Step 2: Support the Planter (Chapter 9)

- Understand and participate in the governing team.
- Provide for planter coaching.
- Develop planter/parent covenant.

Step 3: Allow the Parent Church to Recover (Chapter 9)

- Accelerate the parenting church's health with NCD checkup.
- Address leadership development with mentoring.
- Take time for recovery of attendance, finances, emotions.
- Celebrate successes and understand setbacks.
- Capture learning from parenting experience for next plant.

Parenting Church Values Assessment Tool

Are these characteristics true of your church? Answer "yes" or "no" with your congregation in mind. Churches that have strong parenting values are most likely to experience parenting as a natural expression of their identity. Churches that do not can still parent, but are wise to develop these core values.

1. Compassion for the Unchurched

- ❯ Our church is characterized by investing resources into the lives of people who are not members.
- ❯ We have ministries outside our walls where the message and presence of Jesus are felt.
- ❯ Our congregation has mobilized to meet significant needs in the community.
- ❯ A portion of our church budget is devoted to making a caring impact on the community around us.
- ❯ Our leadership gives considerable time to discern and strategize how to show the love of Christ to our community.

2. Culturally Relevant Style

- ❯ Our ministry style is one that "outsiders" can quickly relate to.
- ❯ The teaching of our church engages seekers and speaks to their needs.
- ❯ The worship of our church is led in a way that engages seekers and speaks to their needs.
- ❯ The visual and stylistic methods of our congregation tend to put "outsiders" at ease.
- ❯ Our ministry attracts new people.

3. Great Commission Orientation

- ❯ Our church often uses new methods to share the good news of Jesus.
- ❯ Our leadership often reminds us of the number of people yet to be reached in our community.
- ❯ Our church never lets money stand in the way of making new disciples.
- ❯ We have a culture in which making new disciples is expected and planned for.
- ❯ In the last year there has been at least one class or sermon series on how to share our faith in a winsome way.

4. Developing and Releasing Leaders

- ❯ Our congregation has a history of raising up new leaders for ministry.
- ❯ We have watched with joy as some of our best leaders move on to new ministry opportunities.
- ❯ There is a "leadership pathway" at our church whereby new leaders are mentored and trained.
- ❯ Our pastors and staff often empower younger leaders and encourage their development.
- ❯ Our church has a ministry in identifying, training, and releasing new ministry leaders.

5. Confidence in God's Ability

- ❯ We have a pattern of making bold plans that depend on God's provision.
- ❯ Our church has often had to rely entirely on God to reach its goals.
- ❯ We dream God-sized dreams and worry about the resources later.
- ❯ Our congregation has stories of how God met needs beyond our dreams.
- ❯ We trust that where God leads, God provides.

6. Kingdom Perspective

- Our leadership seems to care little about who gets the credit as long as the job gets done.
- Our church has partnered with other denominations to do effective ministry.
- Our congregation is focused on people being followers of Christ, not on what denomination they are part of.
- We are not easily threatened by a new church that starts up nearby.
- Our leadership has an "abundance mentality" as far as ministry opportunities are concerned.

7. Generosity

- Our congregation is a giving community. We often raise funds for outside ministries.
- We have committed funds to help plant new ministries outside our walls.
- Our congregation has recruited funds and people to help start a new church.
- We have a history of reaching our funding goals for outreach efforts.
- A percentage of our budget is committed to mission-type efforts.

NOTE: The above questions can be found in an assessment inventory form with a response score option in *Parent Church Landmines* by Ben Ingebretson and Tom Nebel (ChurchSmart, 2009, pp. 93-95).

Appendix C

Planter/Parent Covenant

" . . . so that the sower and the reaper may be glad together." (John 4:36)

I. Commitments of the Parent Congregation to the Planter

a. We will support this effort with prayer and advocacy by

_____

_____

b. We will keep communication open and healthy by

_____

_____

c. We will commit the following resources:

_____

_____

d. We will seek to build trust by

_____

_____

e. Other:

_____

_____

II. Commitments of the Planter to the Parent Congregation

a. I will keep communication open and healthy by

_____

_____

b. I will be accountable to agreed-upon benchmarks by

_____

_____

c. I will seek to build trust by

_____

_____

d. I will honor the support of the parent church by

_____

_____

e. Other:

_____

_____

III. Shared Commitments in Decision Making Relative to

a. *The primary objective, target, and purpose of the plant:*
As parent and planter we commit together to maintain the original intent and purpose of this plant unless we agree otherwise.

b. *The fiscal sustainability of the new church plant:*
As parent and planter we commit to a financial plan and budget that is appropriate and agreeable to both parties.

c. *Staffing evaluation, additions, and eliminations in the new church plant:*
As parent and planter we commit to staffing decisions and evaluation that are the result of due process and shared understanding.

d. We agree to meet monthly to review our progress and our shared commitments.

Signature of Parent Congregation leadership:

_____

Signature of Church Planter:

_____

Church Plant Wish List

The following is a partial listing of resources that will help your plant get off to a strong start:

Planter visibility

1. Regular platform visibility, 2. Preaching and teaching opportunities, 3. Care of a sub-congregation or class, 4. Primary leadership of a highly visible ministry, 5. Highly visible clergy functions (weddings, funerals, baptisms, communion)

Office support

1. Computers, 2. Printers, 3. Copiers, 4. Phones, 5. Supplies, 6. Administrative assistant support as needed.

Office systems

1. Accounting systems, 2. Donor systems, 3. By-laws, 4. Tracking and assimilation systems. 5. Finance person as needed.

Worship resources

1. Instruments; 2. Music scores and sources; 3. Sound systems, microphones, boards, speakers etc.; 4. Lighting systems; 5. Cameras and projectors; 6. Tech and performance personnel as needed.

Sermon preparation resources

1. Books, 2. Commentaries, 3. Language tools, 4. Coaching and support from other experienced preaching pastors.

Furniture

1. Desks, 2. Chairs, 3. Files, 4. Bookcases, 5. Tables, 6. Lights

Children's ministry equipment

1. Cribs, 2. Changing tables, 3. Swings, 4. Climbing toys, 5. Child's tables and chairs, 6. Teaching aids, 7. Craft aids.

Prayer support

1. Prayer teams, 2. Personal intercessors, 3. Corporate prayer, 4. Prayer letter support.

People and leaders

1. Givers, 2. Attendees, 3. Evangelists, 4. Worship leaders and teams, 5. Bible teachers, 6. Youth workers, 7. Children's workers, 8. Nursery workers, 9. Group workers, 10. Office volunteers, 11. Lawyers, 12. Accountants.

Financial gifts

1. Start-up funds, 2. Staff salary, 3. Monthly support, 4. Special projects, 5. Equipment purchases, 6. Stewardship coaching to the planter.

—adapted from *Churches Planting Churches*, Bob Logan and Steve Ogne, Church Smart, 1995, pp. 11-8 – 11-10.

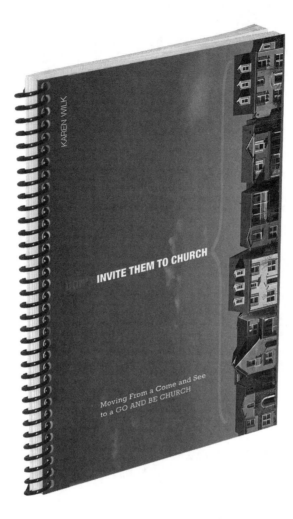

Loving your neighbors isn't about getting them to join you on Sundays. It's about living your faith right where you are and BEING the church to the people around you.

This flexible guidebook will help you, your small group, or your church get started in neighborhood ministry and missional living. It includes ideas for group meetings, practices to help you develop a better spiritual life, and real-life ideas for reaching out to your neighborhood.

FaithAliveResources.org